For Pat
Blessed Trails,
Dee Strickland Johnson

Collector's Edition

Arizona Herstory

Tales From Her Storied Past

Dee Strickland Johnson

Foreword by Marshall Trimble

Illustrations by the Author
and Bridget Heeringa

Arizona Herstory: Tales From Her Storied Past

Edited by Janice Coggin

Publisher: Cowboy Miner Productions
P.O. Box 9674
Phoenix, AZ 85068
Phone: (602) 596-6063
www.CowboyMiner.com

Publisher's Cataloging-in-Publication Data
Johnson, Dee Strickland, 1931—
Arizona Herstory: Tales From Her Storied Past
Dee Strickland Johnson. Edited by Janice Coggin.
p. cm. Illustrated.

ISBN: 1-931725-05-5
1. Arizona History—Poetry. 2. Cowboy Poetry—Arizona.
3. Western History (U.S.)—Poetry 4. Poetry—Arizona Historical
I. Title

Library of Congress Control Number: 2003108111

Book Design & Typesetting: SageBrush Publications, Tempe, Arizona
Jacket Design: Rebecca Johnson Vigon and ATG Productions, Phoenix, Arizona
Jacket Photo: Gerald B. Allen, American West Travelogue http://www.amwest-travel.com
Printing: Bang Printing, Brainerd, Minnesota

Printed and bound in the United States of America

Dedication

To my daughter Becky for designing and maintaining my web site plus immeasurable assistance on this manuscript,

To my husband John for his patience, help, and encouragement over the seven years of loving labor it has taken to complete this book,

And to my sons, Daniel and Tim, for the love and respect they show their mother.

Foreword

As a youngster, I never dreamed I'd grow up to become a History professor, much less the state historian. I didn't care much for history as it was taught to me in high school or even college, for that matter. However, in 1958, I bought an old Gibson guitar for five dollars and became caught up in the folk music craze of the 1950's. The songs I loved most were those of Americas' past. The music took me to places I'd never been and introduced me to the subject of history in a whole new way. I became a history teacher at Coronado High School in Scottsdale and stumbled badly until one day I brought my guitar to class and "laid a few tunes on 'em." The rest is history.

In ***Arizona Herstory***, award-winning writer-performer Dee Strickland Johnson, uses an unusually effective means to bring Arizona's past to the reader—history in verse. Her western poems range from *"Heroes and Hard Cases,"* such as the notorious Buckskin Frank Leslie, to *"Just Plain Folks"* like Tio Pepe, to a section called *"Legends, Lore, Myths and More,"* which includes the tales of La Llorona, and the Peralta Gold in the Superstition Mountains. Each has been carefully researched to make sure the story is told accurately. She weaves songs and poems from documented history, as well as from her own experience as a young girl born and raised on northern Arizona's Colorado Plateau, so some of her tales are of people she has actually known.

Some of these poems will make you laugh, others will tug at your heart strings, while still others have a sense of drama that is as real as the smoke from a Colt .45 or the dust from a herd of cattle. The result is always a mesmerizing story that closely reflects the life and times of those hardy men and women who settled the Old West.

The only thing better than reading Dee's poems is to sit in the audience and watch her perform them. In our little world of cowboy poetry, music and storytelling, she is known as "Buckshot Dot," and is one of the most gifted and talented performers I've ever had the pleasure of working with. "It is my purpose," she wrote, "to help preserve the heritage of the West through traditional songs and original poetry derived from experience and research of the past." In ***Arizona Herstory,*** she has certainly done that.

Marshall Trimble
Official Arizona State Historian

Preface

"A history book in verse?" you may ask, and your next question might well be, "Why?" My reply is simply, *Why not?* Who among us cannot cite the date of the arrival of Christopher Columbus in the New World? "1492, of course!" And why? Because we learned, "In fourteen-hundred and ninety-two, Columbus sailed the ocean blue."

While I seem to have retained nothing from my secondary history classes, I well remember Longfellow's stirring words, "Listen, my children, and you shall hear of the midnight ride of Paul Revere. . ." and, "In Flanders fields the poppies blow between the crosses row on row. . ." by John McCrae, lines which I learned many years before I was in high school. Obviously, history in verse works!

Ask anyone his or her favorite high school subject. Very seldom will the answer be "history". When asked how they liked history, most people seem to reply, "I hated it. All those dates to memorize!" (How sad! The teacher must have been neglecting his homework!)

While teaching American History myself, I quickly learned that innovative methods of presentation made both the teaching and the learning exciting and fun, e.g., the incorporation of poetry, songs, and costumes of the period being studied.

And why *Arizona Herstory* rather than *Arizona History?* Well, it seems that, like all other ships, the ship of our state should be referred to as female—hence it is Her Story (Arizona's). As Arizona came into the Union in 1912, the subject for the 2002 Barry Goldwater Lectures Series was *Arizona: the Old Girl Turns Ninety.* I was invited to appear on this series at Kerr Cultural Center in Scottsdale. Perhaps it was then that the title of this book was determined.

All poems herein are based on actual events—or on what some people believed to have been actual events. Some are straight forward, others tell a serious story in a whimsical manner, but all are a part of Arizona. (It *is* her story).

It is my sincere desire that you, the reader, will find *Arizona Herstory* in verse both interesting and fun, and that you will derive from its reading even a bit of the joy I have had in researching and writing it.

Dee Strickland Johnson

Acknowledgments

The first person whom I should acknowledge is my mother, Anna Beth Strickland, who, by the time of her early death, had instilled in her children the love of art and words, especially poetry, and a deep appreciation for Arizona, the state that brought her solace and healing after the death of her first child in Kansas.

My interest in history originated with a coastguardsman, Carl Nielson, who courted my Aunt Callie in Flagstaff. While waiting for his date, this thoughtful sailor treated a wide-eyed youngster to vivid stories of our nation's past.

Great credit goes to Dr. Patrick Michael Ryan, my thesis advisor, who taught me the intricacies and satisfactions of research and to Ron Kearns, history professor at Scottsdale Community College, who made history so exciting that I switched my area of teaching from drama, English and art to American history.

I wish to express my appreciation to four of Arizona's most respected historians: Dr. James D. McBride, James E. Cook, Marshall Trimble, and Stan Brown for supplying historic information regarding the content of these poems.*

I am indebted to Dr. Robert S. Gray and Barton Wright, for information regarding geology and anthropology respectively, and to Barbara DeSpain, Edna May Patton, Mary Barker, and the Navajo County Historical Society for information on that area of the state. For help with Spanish translation, my thanks to Elke James and Terri Roberts.

Many thanks to J.C. Johnson, Mary Jo Green, and Rebecca Johnson Vigon for proof reading, to Annette Halpern and Bill Lytle for technical assistance and to my publisher—Janice Coggin for her patience and encouragement.

Appreciation is extended to the following persons for answering questions pertaining to historic background and photographs: Dorothy Anderson, Bob Boze Bell, Vince Jenkins, Danette L. Turner, Lorri Carlson, Elaine Filion, Susan Jackson, Robert Mason, Warren Miller, and John A. Swearengin.

Thanks to Jack Burdette for allowing me to print his little commentary on one of my short verses, "Old Soup Bone," and to his wife Katie for believing in me all these years. The following people supplied stories which inspired specific poems: Barbara Baker, Frank Chapman, and Owen Finch. My thanks to them all.

I regret that this book was not finished before the passing of my favorite cowboy Cephas Perkins. He was another great source of inspiration—as is another truly authentic representative of early Arizona, Marguerite Noble.

Dee Strickland Johnson

---

* Dr. James D. McBride, History professor emeritus, Arizona State University.
Marshall Trimble, Arizona's Official Historian.
Stan Brown, Mogollon Rim Country's historian.
Jim Cook, in addition to having been the author of *Arizona Days and Ways* in the *Arizona Republic*, says he is Arizona's Official Liar. (It is important to note that Mr. Cook graciously suspended his Liar's commission when supplying information for this book.)
I wonder if these scholars have yet discovered the disadvantage of being an historian—there's no future in it.

Introduction

This book is intended for the student of Arizona history, as well as for the casual reader of poetry; therefore, unlike most poetry books, it includes copious footnotes.

If you are reading just for the poetry, please ignore all those little numbers at the right side of the page. If, however, you read to learn, I implore you to read the poem straight through once and then go back a second time, in order to explore the subject further by referring to the footnotes.

Certain terms used herein are now considered "politically incorrect" (Indian, Mexican, Darky, Mormon). These were not thought of as offensive at the time in which the poems are set—nor in the days of my childhood. I do not intend them in disrespect. They are used because the modern terms would be anachronistic.

Presenters are welcome to recite my poetry; all I ask is that the author be acknowledged. Some poems are too long to be practical for this purpose. For that reason I have made carefully selected cuts in several poems, which I myself have memorized. These appear in Section Six: Performance Cuts.

We're off to Arizona—it's her story!

Dee Strickland Johnson

Table of Contents

Dates Significant to "Arizona Herstory"

1539 .... Fray Marcus de Niza in Arizona
1540 .... Coronado searches for cities of gold
1598-1607 .. Spanish Colonies established in NM
1608 .... Santa Fe founded
1687-1711 .. Father Kino establishes Missions in Pimeria Alta
Silver strike at Aleh-Shonak
1810-1821 .. Mexican Revolution
1821 .... Mexican independence from Spain
1835-1836 .. Republic of Texas established
1846-1848 .. Mexican War / ended by Treaty of Guadalupe-Hidalgo
1850-1851 ... New Mexico Territory (including Arizona) ceded to U.S.
1853 .... Gadsden Purchase - Arizona gains land south of Gila River
1859 .... Reservation established for Pima and Maricopa Indians (Gila River)
1863 .... Arizona Territory established (Arizona separated from NM)
1861-65 .... American Civil War
1864 .... First Territorial Capital-Prescott
(Original Counties: Yuma, Yavapai, Pima, Mohave)
1865 .... Reservation established for Yumas (Colorado River)
1867 .... Capital moved to Tucson
1868 .... Navajo Reservation established
1871 .... Maricopa County from Yavapai
Apache Reservations established
(Fort Apache and San Carlos)
1874 .... Papago Reservation established San Xavier
1875 .... Pinal County from Maricopa & Pima
1876 .... Territorial prison at Yuma
1877 .... Capital returned to Prescott
Silver strike at Tombstone
1879 .... Apache County from Yavapai
1880 .... Silver and Gold at Jerome
Havasupai Reservation established
1881 .... Cochise County from Pima
Graham County from Pima and Apache
Gila County from Maricopa & Pinal
Southern Pacific railroad crosses southern Arizona
1882 .... Hopi Reservation established

1883 .... Hualapai Reservation established
Atlantic and Pacific railroad crosses northern Arizona
1884 .... Yuma Reservation established
1888-1910 .. Copper at Jerome (replaces gold in Arizona)
1889 .... Territorial capital moved to Phoenix
1889 .... Territorial capital moved to Phoenix
1891 .... Coconino County from Yavapai
1895 .... Navajo County from Apache
1902 .... Yavapai Reservation (Ft.McDowell)
1907 .... Piaute Reservation (Kaibab)
1909 .... Greenlee County from Graham
1911 .... Papago Reservation established
1912 .... Arizona admitted to Union

Map #1: Arizona

This map shows locations of communities mentioned in the poems herein. Some are ghosts towns today.

Map #2

Native Americans of Arizona in Modern Times

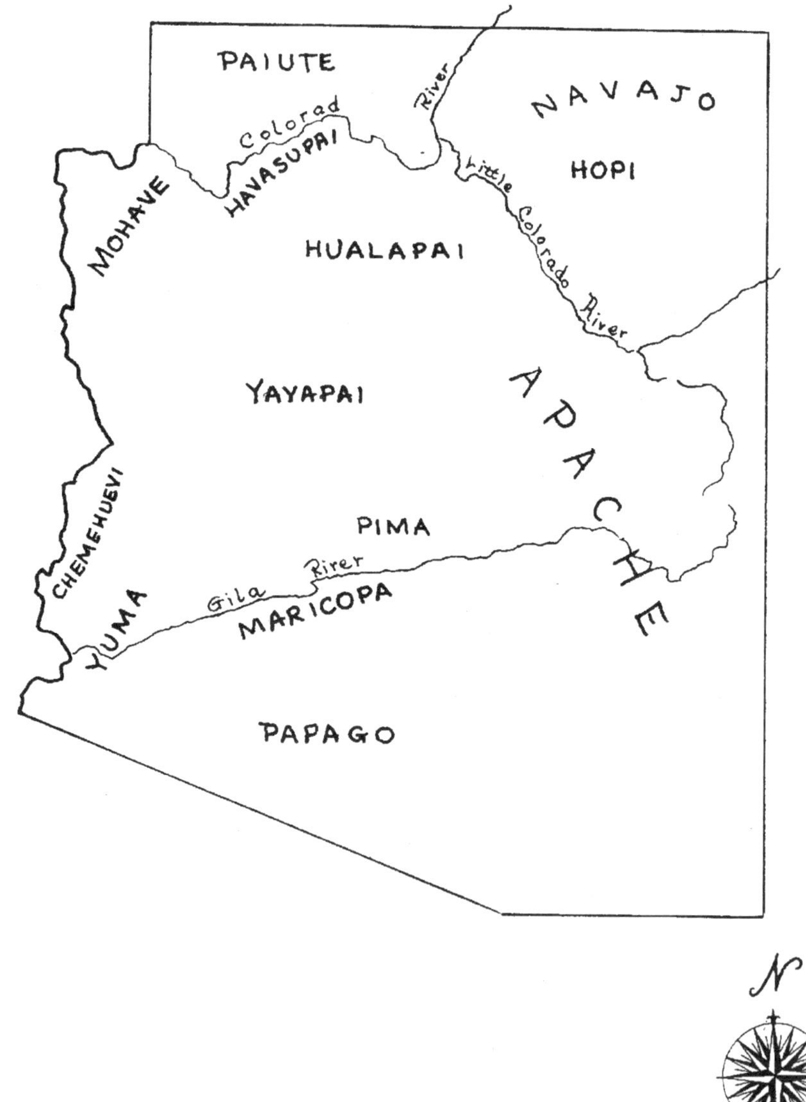

Map #3: Counties—First 100 years (1846-1946)

La Paz was not separated from Yuma until 1983

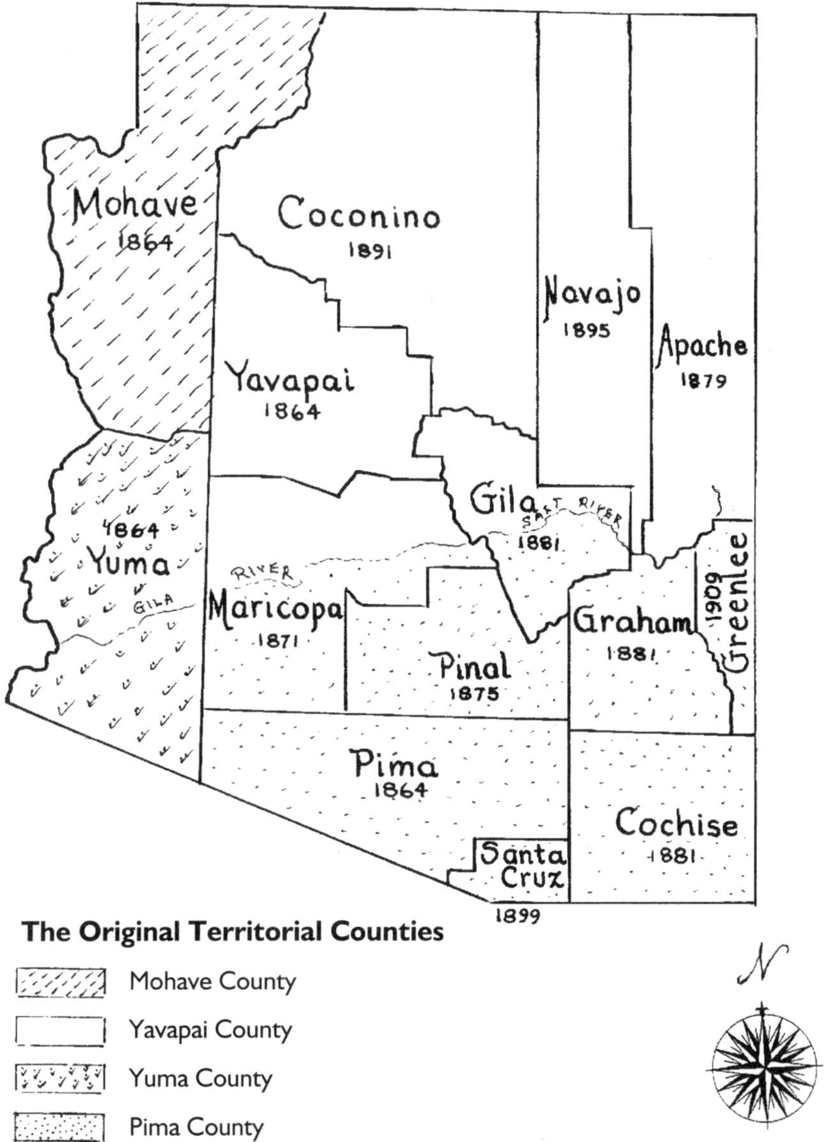

List of Illustrations

Section I: Out of the Mists

Section II: Heroes and Hard Cases

Section III: Just Plain Folks

Section IV: Legends, Lore and More

Section V: Twentieth Century

I. Out of the Mists:
Pre-history to 18th Century

"The old ones scaled the lofty walls and ground their corn in the coolness. . . . They lived there in the morning and when evening came, they were gone."

— Carl King, Mountain View, Arkansas

"No sailor or passenger of the Mayflower yet was born when Arizona greeted its first European tourists; . . . when New Mexico soil drank the blood of its first Old World invader."

— Don Dedera

The Naming of Arizona

ARIZONA: An arid zone;
pretty plain, it seems, but wait!
Historians say that's not the case—
so let's set the record straight.

Wait, I state! Investigate
this fragment of our history,
Lest it may be for you and me
an overwhelming mystery.

In the early Eighteenth Century
Spaniards flocked to a silver find
Near what Papagos called "*Aleh-shona*"[1]
Now, how is *that* defined?

They say *Aleh-shonak*, in Papago
meant, the "*Place of the Small Springs*" . . . well,
It seems I sense a "coincidence"
which the problem may dispel.

Small, you know, means *little*;
Springs: fresh water source.
Thus, *Place of Little Water:* Arid zone.
Arid Zone: Arizona, of course!

Epilogue

The rhythm of "*Aleh-shonak*"
 rolled not soft on the Spanish tongue;
So they called it "*Arizonac*";
 and so it was begun,

This corruption of the Indian words
 the white man changed it then;
Americans said, "Arizona",
 so there we have it, again![2]

---

1) Papagos are now known as the Tohono O'odham.
2) Will C. Barnes, *Arizona Place Names*, ed. Byrd H. Granger (Tucson, 1960), p. xv.

Red Stone Face[1]

We were traveling down the highway
on the way we had to go
Driving back from Colorado one fall day.
It was out where Arizona
gently joins New Mexico,
That we spied the Indian's face along the way.

He had a broad red forehead
and an aquiline strong nose,
And his jaw was jutting forward toward the west.
He was carved by some great chisel
from the media God chose—
That bright vermilion sandstone told it best.

I wonder what the Indian's seen
as the centuries have passed
Before that rugged face, whose sightless eyes
Looked westward o'er high desert—
sandy, stony, sparsely grassed—
No hint of soothing shade or compromise.

Does he view a few young diggers,
walking warily and slow,
Gath'ring rocks to build a simple pit house home?
Does he hear the rumbling thunder
of a herd of buffalo—
Long since vanished from where antelope still roam?

Does he stare off toward the canyons
where the old cliff dwellings clung,
Where men and women
climbed the treacherous walls,
As inverted cross-shaped doorways
neath their skillful hammers sprung[2]
On ledges where there's barely space to crawl?

Some sought to steal their women
    and their tiny stores of food
Coaxed with flint hoes from unsympathizing lands.
Does he watch them clash in battle
    in a never ending feud?
From the north and from the east,
    these roaming bands.

Does he see the tiny patches
    of corn and beans they'd hoed
Trampled 'neath the hooves
    of strange four-footed beasts
That carried light-faced warriors
    who rattled as they rode
And glistened in the sunlight from the east?

Recalls he pious clerics
    garbed in robes of black or brown[3]
Struggling 'gainst the wind,
    the heat, the rain, the snow,
Bearing long carved staffs pastoral,
    with wooden crosses crowned,
While their chained beads rustle softly as they go?

Does he witness spotted ponies
    sweep across the colored hills,
Bearing mounted red-skinned men
    with painted breasts?
Observe the straining oxen
    pull the creaking wooden wheels
Moving awkward covered wagons headed west?

Does he watch the wispy wagon tracks
    become a well-worn trail?
Does he see rough men, with leather faces, weep
As they hollow shallow graves out?
Does he hear the women wail
Leaving children dead
    where winds of winter sweep?

Does old Stone Face see the soldiers
    come in regimental pride?
Does he see them clash with native warrior foes
Who fight and fall and rise again
    and valiantly still ride
Toward a destiny of death and shattered bows?

Does he feel the raindrops streak his cheek?
    Hear ghostly gray wolf's howl?
The cries of eagle, crow, and red tailed hawk?
See *Dineh,* cold and hungry,
    'neath the pale moon of the owl[4]
On the trail to Bosque Redondo—
    their *Long Walk?* [5]

Does he watch great lumbering oxen
    pulling, straining, down the trails?
Does he hear the heavy hammers' ringing blows
As hard men span a continent
    with gleaming long steel rails
That will bring the days of roaming to a close?

Does he see the sputtering model T's
    raise dust—or run amuck,
Followed later by the models A and B?
Observe the roads, now wider,
    fill with ceaseless cars and trucks
As far as his old sightless eyes can see?

Can those eyes make out the jet trails
    slicing, white, across the skies?
Does he sense the clear blue sky is turning gray?
As billowing from smoke stacks,
    fetid clouds and vapors rise
Along the tracks now called the *Santa Fe?*

Sees he machinery digging,
  building houses for the crowds
Who come slashing, burning, tearing at the land?
Do Mother Earth and Father Sky
  cry out in anguish loud
As the Cats keep gouging, scraping at the sand?[6]

Does his memory hold the sounds and sights
  of all he's seen and heard?
Still, staunchly, grim and silent, let him be!
Hush! Did I hear a sighing?
  Could that have been the wind?
It sounds like someone weeping.
No! Not he!

---

1) When one is headed west on I-40, the red stone face is visible on the south side about 4½ miles east of the Arizona-New Mexico border.
2) Such doorways are found in ancient Anasazi dwellings.
3) The Jesuits (Society of Jesus), who wore robes of black, were expelled from the new world by King Carlos III in 1767. They were replaced by the brown robed Franciscans who had first entered Hopi land in 1629.
4) *Dineh*—(Navajo) "the people". The owl, in many Native American traditions, is considered the portent of death.
5) *Bosque Redondo*—The location in northern New Mexico where the Navajos were relocated in January, 1864 in what has been termed *The Long Walk*. Under orders, Col. Kit Carson and his men destroyed everything in their path—hogans, fields, stock, peach orchards. This led to the surrender of eighty five hundred Navajos who were then forced to make the 350 mile march to Fort Sumner where they lived under negligent concentration for four years.
6) Tractors of the Caterpillar Company were called "*Cats*".

Rim of the Mogollon

A dramatic escarpment of cliff cuts diagonally across north central Arizona and western New Mexico from northwest to southeast. This is the Mogollon Rim which marks the departure from the high plateau to the desert below. In between are juniper, piñon, pine, mesquite, etc.

The ancient ones walked softly
Above the canyon's rim
And scaled the walls, and lived their lives,
In ages past and dim.

Shrouded in circling mists of time
Lies the bowl whence came this shard,
This obsidian point, a masterpiece
Wrought in stone—long-lasting, hard.

The bowl was born in a woman's hands
In some lost civilization,
The flint, by the arrow smith's skillful plan,
Acquired its configuration.

But the sands of time have fallen fast
O'er those peoples who went before.
Five hundred years or more have passed
O'er the cliff home's open door.

Did buffalo range o'er the open plains
Of the land of the long since dead?
Ah! I can't constrain the awful pain
Which the shard and the arrowhead

Produce in my mind; for long left behind
Are the minds and the fingers that fashioned
These enduring things—and my heart strings ring
With emotion and compassion.

Lightning bolts flashed as cultures clashed
And the silence was broken asunder.
They fought with a will atop their high hill
And the canyons echoed with thunder;

For, inevitably, the wild and free,
Confronted these invaders,
By some befriended, and together defended
Their primitive lives 'gainst new raiders.

Oh, where have they gone? Now every new dawn
Views a forest of houses new grown.
Is it wind that sighs—or do sad dark eyes
Gaze down from the Mogollon?

Where is the brain from which concept came
for arrow and pottery bowl?
Where the intellect, fingers, and hands,
The spirit, the mind, and the soul?

So I regard the pottery shard;
The arrow point holds me enthralled.
While pale hands, alas, mount them under glass
To adorn "Arizona Room" walls.

---

* Mogollon (Mug-ee-own or Moge-ee-own).

From the statue by Suzanne Silvercruz, Arizona's contribution to Statuary Hall, Washington, D.C. Used by permission of Statuary Hall.

Father Eusebio Francisco Kino

Pioneer Padre on Horseback:[1]
Father Kino in the New World: 1686-1711

Recorded history of the 48th state began with the Spanish Conquistadors and priests entered the land that is now Arizona over four hundred and fifty years ago—nearly seventy years before the English arrived at Jamestown and more than eighty years ahead of the Pilgrims at Plymouth.

Wilderness winds have sifted and shifted
the rolling and restless sand;
O'er crumbling walls it's scattered and drifted,
as years stilled the swift moving hands
Of the man responsible for the walls
of the missions which he had planned,
Bringing cattle, horses, goats, and sheep
to a strange, unchartered land.

He mapped and explored, with care he'd record
the occurrences of his days
In diaries and journals in sessions nocturnal,
while singing Lord Jesus's praise.
Those of the Jesus Society's own
Spain's bright red and gold flag unfurled,
the cross and the crown they bore around
via missions throughout the world.

Struck down in his youth by a dread disease,
He had yielded to fate's two-edged sword:
If he died, he would die in God's good grace,
if he lived, he would live for the Lord.[2]
By "celestial favor" he survived;
became *Eusebio Francis Chino*
(To honor Saint Francis Xavier),
and, ultimately, *Father Kino.*

Born in the green Italian Tyrol,
excelling in science and math,
Kino's heart was bent on the Orient,
but the Lord determined his path.[3]
After long delays in Europe,
where two years he was forced to remain,
He was finally assigned where the Lord had designed:
the mission fields of New Spain.

This pioneer pathfinder, peacemaking priest
did persist to accomplish his goals,
Enduring the dangers, the thirst and the heat,
baptizing and saving souls.
The Pimas rushed to the padre's arms
outstretched in protection and love,
And his missions formed a wall of defense
from Apache strongholds above.[4]

Exploitation of natives, Kino decried;
he succeeded in getting the King
To exempt his Pima "children"
from the harsh and terrible sting
Of slave labor in the mines for Spain
on the Pimas' far frontiers:
A royal cedüla granted reprieve
for a spate of twenty years.[5]

To inspect the work of Kino,
Father Salvatierra came;
He was astonished by the devotion
that followed Fray Kino's name.
The valleys bloomed with abundance,
Pimas traveled for days and hours
To welcome their kindly black-robed priest,
bearing crosses covered with flowers.[6]

The padre put more than eight thousand miles
under his mustangs' feet;
To bring blossoming trees, great purple grapes,
bright fields of golden wheat.
"The west's first cowboys," the Pimas became,
excelling in handling cattle,
Proficient horsemen, they branded and roped
as if they'd been born to the saddle.[7]

Boldly across Pimeria, he strode,
  to his "children," never a stranger.[8]
For twenty-four years, harsh deserts he rode,
  ignoring discomfort and danger;
But never complaint did anyone hear
  from Kino, though other priests grumbled.
He endured, he accomplished, he worked and he died,
"Where lesser men would have crumbled."

To the end of his life, in piety,
  poverty, peace, and the presence of God,
With patience and prayer, persistence and care,
  he hallowed the sandy sod
For the sake of Christ and the king of Spain.
  He fell celebrating the mass.[9]
They carried the beloved dying priest
  to his cell where he'd breathe his last.

When they attempted to lay him down,
  he refused to accept the bed;
So he died on the floor on two sheep skins
  with a pack saddle under his head
In his one black robe and a simple shirt,
  as he'd slept for twenty four years.
The bells tolled somber, long and loud,
  and the desert flowed with tears.[10]

No longer the welcome tread of his boots
  in twenty-four mission yards,
No longer the toll of the great bronze bells
  which the padre had installed;
Yet, down through the years, the faith remains
  after numerous generations
Of those he had lived and died to serve:
  a remote and grateful nation[11]

---

1) The phrase "padre on horseback" appears in "*The Saga of Father Kino,*" by Edwin J. McDermott, S.J. (*ArizonaHighways,* March, 1961, p. 11). It was later used as the title of Herbert Eugene Bolton's well known book on Father Kino (Chicago, 1963).

2) Young Eusebio Chino used the expression "by celestial favor" when referring to his healing, which he ascribed to the mission saint, Francis Xavier. True to his promise, Chino joined the Society of Jesus (Jesuit), taking the name Francis and vowing to go into the mission field for Spain. *(Chino* is pronounced *Kino* in Italian, hence, in New Spain he became known as Father Eusebio Francisco Kino).
3) Kino (Chino) was born August 10, 1645 in the village of Segno and received his education in Austria and Germany.
4) While Kino's missions in Pimeria remained, the threat of Apache attack was largely thwarted. It was his dream to create a chain of missions from Sonora to the Pacific coast, but after his first brief journey into Baja, he was never allowed to return to California, which, by his theory of *blue shells,* he proved, quite conclusively, was a peninsula rather than an island as had there-to-fore been thought. (McDermott, 24).
5) Enslaving the natives was part of the *repartimiento* (apportionment) system. The king who granted temporary immunity for the Pimas was Carlos II. Charles Polzer, S.J. states the length of reprieve was twenty years. *(A Kino Guide,* Tucson, 1968, p.6). McDermott, however, gives the length of immunity as only five years. The *Pima* were comprised of a number of diverse groups. The Spanish are said to have come for "Gold, God, and Glory;" the first priest into this remote area, Fray Marcos de Niza (1539 and 1540), was more an explorer for those seeking Gold and Glory for Spain and themselves than for bringing God to the hapless natives of the region. Kino was truly dedicated to the cause of God.
6) Jealous of Kino's amazing success in Pimeria, some priests started rumors about "quarrelsome Indians in his charge." Father Juan Maria Salvatierra, was originally sent "to the rim of civilization" as Padre Visitador (Visitor General) to review the situation. So impressed was he with what Kino had there accomplished, that he requested and received permissicn to work in that field himself, where he became the "giant of lower California." (Polzer, *A Kino Guide,* p. 7).
7) Although Kino was not the first to bring cattle, horses, mules and other stock into the area, he certainly expanded and improved the industry. For specifics on Kino's contributions, see James E. Officer, *"Kino and Agriculture in the Pimeria Alta," Journal of Arizona History* XXXI:3 (Autumn 1993). 291-295.
8) Their land was known as *Pimeria,* the section in what is now Arizona as *Pimeria Alta* (Upper Pima). (Polzer, op. cit.). Kino was missionary, explorer, cosmographer, geographer, cartographer, architect, contractor, rancher, botanist, farmer and general devoted laborer to Pimeria. (See Bolton, *Padre,* pp. 16, 34, 56 and Officer, *Kino and Agriculture,* pp. 295-300).
9) He had been invited to dedicate a new chapel in honor of his patron saint, San Francisco Xavier, at the Magdalena mission in Sonora.
10) Father Kino died March 15, 1711 at the age of sixty-six. His exact burial spot remained a mystery for many years. It was not until 1966 that its location was rediscovered and confirmed to be in the very capilla (chapel) in which he died.

11) Although some of the missions founded by Father Kino have been rebuilt by the Franciscans who replaced the Jesuits in 1767, others lie in complete ruin. The dearly loved Padre had established twenty-four missions and nineteen ranches in what is now northern Sonora and southern Arizona. His parish covered over 50,000 square miles into which he made over 50 journeys. His mission buildings are long since gone; yet, Father Kino remains deeply venerated throughout Pimeria. Its people "still revere his shadow, his cross and his bell," (McDermott, p. 29) and continue to name their sons Francisco, Xavier, Eusebio, and Kino in his honor.

Kino's Object Lesson

Father Kino diligently tried to teach
the concept of resurrection:
He stunned some flies, so that they would revive,
then allowing some time for reflection,
Told his translator to put it in the tongue
of his "children"—the lesson he'd brought.
He later discerned the words they had learned:
"Ellos son muertos" (they're dead), they'd been taught.

If Anza Had Remained

When English colonists arrived at Jamestown in 1607 and at Plymouth in 1620, the Spanish Empire was already thriving in western America. Arizona was originally a part of the province of New Mexico, begun in 1598, as was the southern part of Colorado. In 1774, Captain Juan Bautista De Anza organized the expedition described in this poem.

America's colonization, so the history books attest,
Was due *English* ingenuity, manifested East to West;
Some slight mention of *French* trappers,
in furs and leather dressed,
Who followed the rivers North to South;
but here in the great Southwest,

A great *Spanish* culture had flourished long,
with gold and God obsessed
To subdue and convert the natives
at the cross and the crown's behest.
Juan Bautista De Anza,
a soldier one day would be,
Like his grandsire, and his father
who died when Juan was three
In an awful Apache ambush of the Spanish cavalry.

At eighteen, Juan joined the army;
only six years later, he,
The youngest captain in all New Spain,
the Commandante proved to be
Of the presidio at Tubac
where the fearful fierce Apache
Remained an ever-present threat.
Those dauntless renegados,
Most feared of all the Indians
from Sonora to Colorado,
Would steal the Spanish horses—
why, entire *caballados!*[1]

The title "Indian Fighter"
soon graced young Anza's name,
For fearless and resourceful,
the young commander came
To dispel the feared Apache—
this became the young man's aim.
The good padre, Father Garces,
of the California missions,[2]
Had scouted the Colorado's course
and with typical ambition,
Saw an overland route was possible
and prepared an exposition

To link Sonora to California!
Juan Bautista secured permission
From the viceroy, himself to lead
this hazardous expedition
On *Camino del Diablo*,[3]
and despite adverse conditions,
Crossed the mighty Colorado
and returned with a new commission:
To colonize California,
and despite some opposition,
Convinced military families
to come of their very own volition.

Thirty soldiers, wives and children,
two priests and an Indian guide,
Two hundred and forty valiant souls
with the Captain's plan complied.
They traveled to Yuma crossing,
and upon him there relied.
At the confluence of two rivers,
where the Quechan people dwell,[4]
Captain Anza's previous journey
had prepared the way quite well,
He'd calmed the suspicious Indians
and their grave mistrust dispelled.

He gained access to the crossing,
    there the Captain did foretell
A mission at this very spot, complete with citadel.[5]
He truly meant that it would be.
    Travelers crossed, then, safe and well.
So, in seventeen hundred seventy six,
    they reached San Gabriel,[6]
Where they were welcomed, one and all,
    by the tolling of the bell.
There the Captain left his charges,
    bidding all a fond farewell.

He hastened North to select a site
    for presidio and mission
To be called *San Francisco*,
    But received, then, recognition
As Governor of New Mexico,
    continuing his tradition
    as benevolent *soldier-statesman,*
Status changer by definition.
Thus, Anza set to his new job,
    to hostilities no stranger,
From hostile bands of Apaches, still,
    New Mexico was in danger;

He took on the ominous Indians
    Of the Colorado plains,[7]
Defeating the wild Comanches,
    Set the others once again
To fighting *one another*—
    a victorious campaign! [8]
But his promises to the Quechan?
    Well, they were all in vain.
Though they were meant in best of faith,
    the ministers of Spain
Did not see fit to follow through,
    so Anza could not attain

A mission for the Yumas,
 and in seventeen eighty one
They revolted! Juan De Anza's work
 most grievously undone.
That strategic river crossing
 was open now to none
Of Spanish blood; hence, hundreds
 of Spaniards there were slain.[9]
Our country might have built west to east;
 our ways, be the ways of Spain;
Our history books might have read differently,
 Had Anza but remained!

---

1) Caballado: Horse herd.
2) In 1767, King Carlos III expelled the Jesuits from the Spanish realm in the new world, replacing them with the Franciscans. The route followed by Anza and the Franciscan padre, Father Francisco Tomas Garces had been suggested by the Jesuit Father Eusebio Kino years earlier. Kino had established the Arizona missions and determined, in 1699, that California was not an island and could, therefore, be reached by an overland route.
3) Camino del Diablo: The Devil's Highway. It probably was not called by this name until after the end of the Mexican War in 1848, although Kino had taken the route several times. The trail moved from Sonoita, to Yuma on the Colorado River. One branch moved north and followed the Gila River for some distance before continuing to the Colorado crossing. Father Garces accompanied Anza on two of his expeditions across the Colorado.
4) *Two rivers:* The Colorado and Gila.
 Quechan people: Yuma Indians.
5) The Quechan Chief Palma was taken to Mexico City where he was treated royally. He was baptized there and many promises were made to him and his people, including the construction of a mission at Colorado crossing.
6) San Gabriel is near what is now Los Angeles. Actually, Anza did not agree with the mission concept. In his report of December 15, 1772, he wrote, "With regard to the advancement of these heathens . . . I say that the surest way to attain the worthy goals . . . is to destroy and reform the system up to now observed in the mission. . . . I believe that (the Indians) should be left in complete possession of what is theirs to work for themselves for their own benefit. They should not be forced to do it for the community . . . ." *Soldier's Criticism of Indian Policy, 1772." Journal of Arizona History,* XIII:1, p. 59.

7) Anza's army defeated the Comanche leader Cuerna Verde (Green Horn) in Colorado. This ended the threat of the Comanches in New Mexico. "A treaty was made with the Comanches that lasted long after the Americans . . . gained possession of the land." It was "a significant tribute" to Anza's diplomatic abilities. (Marshall Trimble, *Arizona Adventure!* [Phoenix, 1996], p. 25).
8) The Navajos and Apaches resumed fighting each other.
9) The transfer of Anza to New Mexico in 1778 was a fatal mistake for the Spanish. Anza warned that benevolent treatment of Indians, especially those at river crossings, was crucial, but subsequent military leaders and soldiers dealt harshly with the natives, and promises were broken. As a result, in 1781 Chief Palma led his Quechan people in revolt at the Yuma Crossing. Among those killed in this rebellion was the kindly old Franciscan priest Father Garces.

From a photograph in *True West* Archives. Courtesy Bob Boze Bell, Editor.

Yuma (Quechan) Indians

II. Heroes and Hard Cases: Nineteenth Century

Poems are arranged in approximate chronological order, with indication of the general area in which the events took place.

"Lives of great men all remind us we can . . .
leave behind us footprints in the sands of time."

— Henry Wadsworth Longfellow

"There's nothing nicer than a charming outlaw."

— Rebecca Johnson Vigon, Mineral, Virginia

The Battle of Picacho Pass: April 1862

"Although a very small event in a very big war, the 'Battle of Picacho Pass', with its memorials and its stories, establishes Arizona's involvement in America's Civil War."[1]

I. The Scene

On the Arizona desert
 stands a grim and silent peak
That rises stark against the sky,
 and old timers often speak
Of its mystery and prominence.
 They say since time began,
Its majesty and grandeur
 have inspired both beast and man
To climb its steep foreboding slopes
 to stand and look below.
Still, they claim, the sounds of battle
 can be heard when Spring winds blow.

Who knows what wars were fought there
 since earth's dawn was first begun?
Yet, chronicled in history books,
 we know of only one;
But before those guns were crafted
 of which white man's books relate,
Bare feet have sought its comfort
 in the days which knew no date.
There cupped brown hands
 have quenched the thirst
  of those beside its springs
Who knelt to drink and languish
 in the cool of autumn evenings.
Native peoples, Spanish padres,
 soldiers—brown and white and black,
Renegados, desperados
 roaming north and south and back,
Miners, cowboys, Mormon pilgrims—
 all have lingered in its shade,

And the black snake cracked across the backs
of the mounts of the Butterfield Stage
As it passed the silent sentinel;
Then the rumbling ribboned rails,
The tracks of the mighty railroad
passed right near its dusty trails.

Hear the muffled songs the wind sings.
Listen now, for old time's sake,
As deceptive desert's rising heat
conjures up a peaceful lake:
Green Grow the Lilacs, Chisholm Trail,
Sweet Lorena, Aura Lee.[2]
Sharp, urgent muted bugle calls.
Ghostly guns bark soundlessly!

II. A Confederate Plan, 1861-62:

It all began, a pompous plan
in the mind of Major Sibley,
A Confederate army officer,
who explained his scheme quite glibly
To President Jefferson Davis.
This proposal he did confide:
Gold and silver. Seaports.
New recruits he could provide
Were he allowed to venture west
to New Mexico Territory
(Of which Arizona was a part);
O, he told a thrilling story

Of Sonora and California,
from whence volunteers would flock
To join the glorious Rebel cause![3]
Surely, England would take stock,
Recognize the situation,
Then denounce the North's aggression;
And hail the cause of the stars and bars—
the Southern states' secession!
Sibley received approval
from President Davis, and then
He went riding off to New Mexico
with twenty six hundred men.

From AHS photograph #28440. Courtesy of the Arizona Historical Society/Tucson.

Colonel John R. Baylor, CSA
"Governor and Lt. Col. Of Arizona Territory, Confederate States of America"

Half were sent west to Tucson.
    (Sing praises to the South!)
The Texans were as welcome
    as a good rain after drought,
For Apaches surrounded Tucson,
    and the citizens lived in fear:
"Thank God!" they cried, "for the boys in gray—
    Once again we have soldiers here!"
U.S. troops had been withdrawn
    when the southern states seceded,
And settlers in the great Southwest
    most desperately needed

Protection from Apaches.
    Mail, too, had been suspended.
So feelings ran against the north,
    toward Southern causes tended.[4]
In fact, in August '61
    Arizona was declared
A Confederate Territory.
    Now the Rebels were prepared![5]
It was to fool the Union,
    Sibley divided his troops that way.
The second half he headed north—
    to the town of Santa Fe,

The capital of New Mexico.
    Meanwhile, a communiqué
Had been sent to Union forces
    to prepare for a great soiree;
Hence, the *California Column*
    was dispatched without delay:
Two thousand hardy young volunteers
    preparing for the fray.[6]

Heading the Californians,
    Colonel Carlton, on his gray,[7]
Cried, "We must retake New Mexico!
    We must prepare the way!"

He sent McLeave and nine good men
to a place called Ammi's Mill[8]
To select a site to cache supplies
and, that done, continue still
Until they reached old Tucson
to destroy the Rebel stronghold.
A plan for the bravest soldiers!
(So McLeave's men had been long told).

But Confederate Captain Hunter,
of the Tucson occupation,[9]
Heard of the Californians' plan
and quickly left his station;

Proceeded north to Ammi's Mill,
and there carried out his plan:
He changed into civilian clothes
to impersonate the man
Who owned the mill. As *Ammi White,*
Captain Hunter there did wait
Till McCleave and his men approached him.
(The Federals took the bait!)
"The miller" spoke of their uniforms;
said that he had long admired
The blue and gold of the Union dress,
then casually inquired

About the Federal troopers.
McLeave told him they were few,
That the major body would arrive
within a day or two.
Then Hunter, drawing his pistol
as fast as the eye could see,
Pronounced the soldiers prisoners
of the great Confederacy!

III: The Battle, April 15, 1862

Knowing an army was coming,
Hunter headed back over the trail
Which had been used by the Butterfield Stage
for passengers and mail,
Toward the "Old Pueblo" (Tucson),
still held by Confederate troops,
To prepare for the confrontation
of the two determined groups.
He had left nine men at Picacho,
under Sergeant Holmes' command;[10]
This Federals learned from Pima scouts
of the small Confederate band.[11]

James Barrett, with a dozen men,[12]
was to circle 'round behind
The small Rebel band at Picacho,
till, with Union force combined.
They'd advance from the other direction.
Victory seemed assured!
They could all sweep down on Tucson
and the Rebels be disinterred.
Brash and brave, without support,
the Union Lieutenant attacked
The Confederate encampment.
Now men who ride a-horseback

Are easy targets against the sky
for snipers in the brush.
Three Union soldiers toppled,
and one who died in the rush
Was the valiant Lieutenant Barrett,
and three more, wounded, fell
Plus two Confederate casualties
in ninety three minutes of hell.
The Rebels retreated to Tucson;
the Feds to their major force,
After laying their fallen comrades
in their shallow graves, of course.

They say it was merely a "skirmish"
    but for those who died that night,
'Twas the last and most violent battle,
    the final ferocious fight.
And who can say what might have been
    had Confederates, with their plan,
Won New Mexico, California
    Sonora, Chihuahua. and then
Baja and Colorado—
    all the gold and wealth; therefore,
Brave volunteers and England's hand—
    might the South have won the war?

"The Westernmost Civil War battle"
    occurred in eighteen sixty two.
Soon Confederates left the dry Southwest,
    Now neither soldiers gray or blue
Remained of opposing armies.
Settlers turned again to fight
    the Comanches and the Apaches;
Still, they say, on the darkest nights,
    One can hear the clashing troopers,
The rattle of spurs and bits,
    the crack of rifles and anguished cries
        Like a wounded man emits.

Yes! Roaming about Picacho,
    'mongst the mesquite and gamma grass;
    Are the restless souls who played the roles—
        and fell at Picacho Pass!

---

1) L. Boyd Finch. "Sanctified by Myth,The Battle of Picacho Pass," Journal Of Arizona History, XXXVLI: 3, (Autumn 1995), 264.

2) Songs popular during the Civil War.

3) Henry Hopkins Sibley, an officer in the Union army, resigned his commission at the beginning of the war to support the Southern cause, where he became a Confederate General. The objective of the Confederacy in this plan "was to capture the Territory of New Mexico . . . and hold it as a gateway to California. There were even plans for annexation of the Mexican states of Sonora, Chihuahua, and Baja California as outlets for slavery." (A. Blake Brophy, *Fort Fillmore, N.M., 1861:"Public Disgrace and Private Disaster," the Journal of Arizona History,* IX:4, [Winter 1968], 200.

4) Occupied with the war in the East, "the Government of the United States abandoned the first settlers of Arizona to the merciless Apaches." (Boyd Finch, "*Sherod Hunter and the Confederates in Arizona,*" *The Journal of Arizona History*,X: 3 [Autumn 1969], p. 147).
5) New Mexico Territory, at this time, included all of what are now the states of New Mexico and Arizona, as well as portions of Nevada and Colorado. On August 1, 1861, John R. Baylor was appointed "Gov. and Lieut. Col." of "Arizona Territory, Confederate States of America." The suggestion had been made to divide the territory east and west along the 34th parallel (rather than north and south as it is today). Baylor declared this officially done in February 1862, and Mesilla was pronounced the capital of Arizona Territory, the southern half.
6) U.S. troops were headed eastward anyway, as their orders were to go where war was raging—the Southeastern states.
7) U.S. Army Colonel James Carlton.
8) Captain William McCleave, USA.
9) Captain Sherod Hunter, CSA. Before joining the Confederate ranks, Hunter had owned a farm in the Mimbres Valley near Mesilla. After the withdrawal of U.S. troops, he and other white settlers were forced to give up their holdings due to increased Apache attacks. The Indians apparently believed they had driven the army out, and, hence, intensified their efforts to rid the Southwest of what was left of the whites.
10) Sgt. Henry Holmes, CSA.
11) Finch contends that it was "Old mountain man Paulino Weaver." riding point, who spotted the Rebels and warned Union Captain William P. Calloway of the advancing Confederates.
12) Lt. James Barrett, Co. A, First Cavalry Volunteers, USA.

From a photograph in Library of Congress Archives, Washington, D.C.

Col. James H. Carlton, USA Commander of California Regiment

The Gold and Fleece

The Robber

In eighteen hundred and seventy five,
  Widow Jane with sons William and Dan
Were shortly joined by three other sons:
  namely, Riley and Moses and John.

The Casners, they say, were from Oregon way,
  up near Flagstaff, intending to stay,
Bringing large flocks of sheep and confidence deep,
  though John headed on Texas way.

Their stock business prospered,
  and sale of the sheep
    the spring of the following year,
Netted $6,000 plus a bit more;
  but having no handy banks near,

Brother William took charge;
  twenty dollar gold coins
    he placed in a tough buckskin bag,
And thinking his cache a deep secret, one day
  his security happened to lag.

Hired man, Clancey, discovered the gold,
  and that day, playing sick, stayed in camp,
While the brothers themselves went out with the flock,
  sly Clancey lay moaning—the scamp!

Clancey said to the Navajo boy tending camp,
  "Go for water while I go to sleep!"
But the youth, looking back,
  saw the man with the sack
    which held money received for the sheep.

The boy sprinted off, his friend William to find.
 but by the time the two had returned,
Clancey was gone and so was the gold—
 all the money the Casners had earned!

The brothers rode out in hasty pursuit,
 determined to capture their prey!
He might well have escaped, for he had a head start,
 except for the haphazard way

He had hurriedly tied the bag filled with gold,
 (secured only by long saddle strings),
As he'd leapt to his horse, unmindful, of course,
 of such seemingly trivial things.

The strings could not hold the weight of the gold;
 the bag fell to soft needled ground.
A meteorite in his headlong flight,
 the thief heard not one single sound!

When he, reaching back,
 found that he'd lost the sack,
  fast, the outlaw, reversing his steed,
Like a wild maniac, came hurtling back
 whence he'd last felt the prize of his greed.

Twice he slid to a stop, stacked a pile of rocks
 where he thought the bag might have been lost
On the dark forest floor, then dashed on once more,
 but his search far too much time had cost!

Yes, alas for the crook, the Casners o'ertook
 their erstwhile "sick" hired hand,
Lashed him by his coat to a stout black jack oak
 while continuing to demand

He reveal the stash of their hard garnered cash,
but the outlaw just couldn't say;
So they lowered him down and took him to town,
seeking justice by some other way.

The weeks dragged along, and the four Casner boys
continued to work with their sheep,
But they failed to appear when the time drew near
for the trial of the gold from the fleece.

So Clancey went free and boasted that he
had the money still hidden away,
"Forget the affair! It's mine!" he declared,
"And I'll spend every cent my own way!"

And then, strange to say, 'twas reported one day,
both William and Daniel found murdered
Midst the weeds and the rocks where they tended their flocks.
Tragic the fate of the herders!

Once Moses was forced to traverse a course
barefooted through live coals of fire;
But he could not reveal where the gold was concealed—
the thing his tormentors desired.[1]

The years rolled on still, as time always will,
and the gold had still never been found,
Though many had searched 'midst the aspen and birch.
o'er the leafy and pine needled ground.

The Saints Come Rolling In

It was in the same year as the robbery
that a small group of staunch Mormons came.
With their wagons and carts and their stalwart hearts,
They ventured from Utah to claim

A share of the high Arizona plateau.
The Order they called themselves;[2]
And one found his work in the store as a clerk
stocking the company shelves. [3]

Locy Rogers by name; he had little to claim:
a few sheep, a young wife, a small child
And one on the way. Six years later, one day
(for July, the weather was mild),[4]

While tending his flock he received quite a shock—
for there midst the fallen oaks' grime,
Looking dirty and old were coins of pure gold
dulled by weather and fire and time!

The remains of a seamless buckskin sock
lay decaying amongst the gold.
Just a few feet away from a pile of rocks
all covered with dark, leafy mold.

Locy'd heard the tales told of the curse of the gold:
Was his finding some terrible omen?
"Surely this is the gold from that robbery bold
That I hold in my hands at this moment!"

By dawn's early light, Locy planned to take flight,
his mind all filling with dread
About the gold poked down the sleeves of his coat
and the bandits that danced in his head.

He took out his shovel and started to dig
  Before turning in for the night;
With the coins in a hole beneath his bedroll,
  He tossed 'neath the stars' meager light.

At his home, in the ground he hid what he'd found,
  And to only one person confided.
"Go get the Casners!" He told his good friend,
  Who rode to where Casners resided.[5]
He returned with Moses and Riley, who cried,
  "This gift must have come from the Lord!"
Still unbelieving, and scarcely conceiving,
  "How much do you want as reward?"

They could scarcely believe Locy Rogers' reply,
  "Not a thing. I just did what was right."
But a handful of gold, so the story is told,
  They tossed back and rode into the night.

When The Order gave o'er in 1884,
  Rogers moved "up the country," to make[6]
A new home; quite soon he was known,
  As the "Abraham Lincoln of Snowflake".

---

1) Moses suffered the rest of his life as a result of this torture at the hands of would-be robbers.
2) The United Order of Two Hundred, led by Lot Smith, was sent by Brigham Young to settle along the Little Colorado River in Arizona in 1876.
3) This was the official church-owned store of the Zion Company.
4) Rogers found the gold in July, 1882, six years to the month after the robber had dropped it.
5) The Casner ranch was on Oak Creek.
6) The Snowflake, Showlow, Springerville area was referred to as "up the country".

From a photograph in the Rogers family collection. Courtesy Danette L. Turner, great granddaughter of Locy Rogers

Andrew Locy Rogers

Unluckiest Cuss

This is one of those stories that is based on fact, but as there were no newspapers in the vicinity at the time, may be mixed with legend. It is a tale relating to the Copper Queen mine, the claim on which Bisbee was founded. The race, referred to herein, took place at Charleston, near Tombstone, in late 1879 or early 1880.

You've probably heard of the *Lucky Cuss,*
the vein that Ed Schieffelin scratched out;
'Twas the quail that laid the big silver egg,
the egg from which Tombstone was hatched out.

But for every miner that struck it rich,
there were hundreds who dug for naught,
They "tunneled, hydrauliced and cradled" all right[1]
but found little the gold that they sought.

They scrabbled, dabbled and grubbed at their claims,
and they sluiced around with a pan,
But all that it got was wet pants and boots
For many a prospecting man!

But maybe the man most deserving of fame,
as the dang *unluckiest cuss*
(Or maybe *the dumbest)*, was one by the name
of George Warren. Ask any of us!

One night George agreed to a foot race, you see.
(You will scarcely believe it, Señor!)
Foot race, it is true, with George on his *two,*
his opponent, a *horse,* having *four!*

Now, this is how it all came about:
    George's name was on promising claims.
(*How* promising, he could scarcely have known:
    one ninth of the great Copper Queen!)

G.W. Atkins, a partner, they say,
    was "befriending" George, buying the drinks,
When George agreed to the race with a horse.
    (The plot thickens here, Sir, me thinks!)

Warren's share in the Queen against Atkins' horse,
    now, those were the stakes they agreed on.
They'd start by the gun, round a pole, then rerun;
    These, the terms that they wrote the decree on.

Townspeople hurried on out to the track
    that had been laid out for the race.
The distance was marked, and the pole had been set;
    both the man and the horse were in place.

George *actually* outran the horse, it is true,
    on the first leg—from start to the stick!
But after the turn, the horse bolted back
    and won the race mighty darn quick!

That should be the end of this ludicrous tale,
    how George lost a fortune by running
An ill fated race twixt himself and a horse,
    (Or was it G.W.'s cunning?)[2]

But sadly, that's not where the last curtain fell.
    (That would have been much more humane),
But G.W. Atkins petitioned the court,
    proclaiming that George was insane

And "dangerous!" *Dangerous to whom?* you may ask.
To the man who robbed him of his share
In the great Copper Queen, and who sold it forthwith,
Reaping well from the seedy affair

With George in an institution—
an asylum for the insane
Way off in far California.
(The plot now seems pretty darn plain).
In a few years, George was declared fully "healed"
and that was undoubtedly when
He learned that his *guardian* had sold all his claims
(and never was heard from again.)[3]

If that doesn't prove the *unluckiest cuss*
was George Warren, my purpose shall fail.
He died drunk, in a ditch along Brewery Gulch—
That surely must end our sad tale.

But no, it does not, George was honored at last
(Though, sadly, too late for his knowing).
The mining district and town were named
Warren—now that's quite a showing!

Yet, still another tribute remains:
Perhaps George's copper corona
Is that he's the miner who leans on his pick
On the Great Seal of Arizona![4]

---

1) "Tunneled, hydrauliced and cradled": Folk song, *Acres of Clams.*

2) The amount that Warren actually lost was about $150,000, much less than the $20 - $40 million often claimed, but still a great deal of money in the 1880s. (Gary Dillard, *"The Legend of George Warren, Arizona's Unluckiest Prospector," Cochise County History Magazine* (May 1997), pp. 10-17.

3) When Warren was committed to an asylum in Stockton, California, George Pridham was declared his guardian. Had he and Atkins made an arrangement, or was each working individually to pad his own nest with bright copper feathers?

4) The photograph of Warren from which the figure on the Great Seal was drawn, was taken by Tombstone's respected photographer C.S. Fly, sometime in the 1880s.

From a photograph by C. S. Fly in the Crockell collection.
Courtesy Bisbee Mining and Historical Society.

George Warren

What Goes Around . . .

George Warren once held in his hand a goodly portion of the richest copper mine in Arizona, but he let it slip through his fingers. This is the story of how, in 1877, Warren acquired his claim to the mine that was to become the famous Copper Queen in the first place.

I've heard life's a circle and what a man sows,
surely, that shall he also reap,
That the deeds he has done
under day's brilliant sun,
will rob him of many night's sleep.

In that case, Atkins may well have died
from lack of repose, it would seem,
And Pridham, the *guardian* of George Warren, too.
(Their misdeeds were in the extreme.)[1]

Could that be the reason George Warren is called
Arizona's *unluckiest cuss*?
Perhaps we should look at the years in between
those that have been recorded for us:

After the close of that "late greatest war,"[2]
troops were dispatched to *way out in the west*
To end the threat of the Indian raids,
as Apaches could surely attest.

A scouting party from Fort Bowie came,
and camped at a place nature'd hollowed;
At a site that the soldiers called Iron Spring,
for the water could scarcely be swallowed.[3]

Then their scout, Jack Dunn, was duly dispatched[4]
up into those rugged Mule Mountains,
To locate water and transport it back,
supplementing the Iron Spring fountains.

While thusly engaged, some unusual rocks
caught Jack Dunn's analytic attention.
He, to Rucker and Byrne, his friends
showed his find.
Did they think them worthy of mention?

When the rock was assayed, it proved to be *float,*[5]
from some silver outcropping up higher.
Then the partners, Dunn, with Rucker, and Byrne,[6]
agreed it was time to acquire

Someone to grub stake for locating more claims[7]
in the area they'd been inspecting.
(Somehow the army did not take too well
to its men in the hills, off prospecting).

'Twas there at Fort Bowie, they met with a man,
quite well known for his mountaineering.
They trusted George Warren to locate and file
any claims that might be appearing.

George located claims but, by some *quirk of fate,*
his partners names failed to include
When they were recorded,
though they'd staked him well,
providing his tools and his food.

Years later, when George was *no longer insane,*
    and emerged from the madhouse at last,
He became the town's cheerful never-do-well,
    telling tales of his colorful past

To anyone who would buy him a drink
    (He could not earn his own bread and butter);
And so, passed out cold, he was rescued one night,
    being found, dead drunk, in the gutter.

To the hospital then a young traveler brought
    the drunken old alligator,
And himself paid the bill for the sorry old sot
    who expired a few days later.[8]

Warren never found out the young man's name,
    yet, he died, a true creditor
Of the kindhearted son of the scout Jack Dunn
whom *George* had wronged fifteen years earlier.

Yet another coincidence life's blacksmith struck
    At the anvil of fate's fateful forge:
All: Atkins and Pridham, who brought Warren down,
    Himself and his savior—named *George.*

---

1) As recounted in the previous poem and footnotes, Atkins was the partner who got Warren drunk, then talked him into a footrace with Atkins' horse. It was Pridham, George Warren's court appointed legal guardian, who, while Warren was in the asylum, sold all of Warren's remaining mining claims and disappeared with the resulting plunder. (Dillard, 17).
2) America's Civil War was often referred to, particularly in the South, as "The Late Great War".
3) Iron Spring is at the foot of Tombstone Canyon, then called Mule Gulch.
4) Dunn was a civilian scout with Company C, Sixth Cavalry, one of many such units sent West to trail Apaches through the deserts and rugged mountains of Eastern Arizona.
5) *Float* is a piece of mineralized rock that has traveled away from the main ore body. (Janice Coggin, letter to the author, April, 2002).

6) Lt. John Anthony "Tony" Rucker and T.D. Byrne, enlisted man. Rucker was the highly respected young commander of Company C who died a few years later attempting to save the life of a fellow officer in a flooded river. As Dunn had named a mine in another area after himself, this claim was recorded as the *Rucker*. It was the first mine claim in the Bisbee area and became known as the *Copper Queen*.
7) *Grub staking* entailed providing sufficient supplies to allow a prospector to remain in remote areas for an extended length of time. This constituted a partnership agreement. In this case, the original partners lost out, but Warren quickly acquired another grub stake while drinking in a saloon—the new partners were those who would eventually destroy him.
8) George Warren died of pneumonia from exposure to the elements after lying drunk in the ditch during inclement weather. Cheater and cheated, deceiver deceived, this man, who might have lived in luxury, died in poverty.

George Warren: Background

George Warren was born somewhere between 1835 and 1849 in Massachusetts. Following the death of his mother and the aunt who kept him thereafter, George went to join his father Charlie Warren, a teamster, in Arizona Territory. They were tending a government horse herd when attacked by Apaches. The following poem may shed some light on the reason George agreed to the fateful foot race recounted in Unluckiest Cuss.[1]

George lost his mother when he was a child,
saw Apaches slaughter his Daddy,
Was wounded himself in that Indian attack,
seemed his whole life was turning out badly.

He was young, so the Indians took him alive,
and they turned him into a slave,
George learned a lot of Apache ways then,
And that attack, he just never forgave.

He found he could outrun the Indian mules,
Which may truly have had some bearing
On the crazy wager he made later on
which would bring him almost to despairing.

It was fifteen pounds of sugar, he claimed,
That was traded for him (that's the story)
By prospector whites who traveled one night
In that dangerous territory.

He later became an army scout,
and the soldiers thought George had gone mad,
For he killed seven Indians and took all their scalps.
(They were those who had murdered his Dad).[2]

---

1) The wide disparity in birth dates makes it impossible to estimate the year of George's escape from the Indians, the race, etc. Warren believed he had been about nine years old when he arrived in Arizona, and around seventeen when captured by the Apaches. He may, then, have been in his mid forties when the fateful race was run. (Dillard, p. 14).
2) Because of his familiarity with Apacheria and his knowledge of Apache life, Warren was hired as an army scout, but the taking of the Indian scalps did not set well with the military, so George wandered on into other pursuits.

"Johnny Behind the Deuce"

Wyatt Earp earned a considerable reputation as a lawman in Tombstone, the highlight of his career being the altercation with the Clanton "Cowboys" faction; however, many historians view the following episode with a small time gambler as Wyatt's finest hour. It took place on January 28, 1881.

The protagonist of this story
wasn't named *Johnny* at all,
Though the name won him fame and sad glory,
he was *Michael O'Rourke*, rightly called.

He acquired the unique appellation
as result of the practice employed
If his hole card turned out to be a *two,*
and the singular luck he enjoyed!

They called him *Johnny Behind-the-Deuce*;
he'd bet high when he turned up a *two,*
But in January 'eighty-one,
it seemed that his luck was all through.

Now stories vary, as stories will,
about what transpired that day
In Charleston (just east of Tombstone)
at Smith's restaurant: a *fracas they* say,

Though some called it a *disagreement*,
hot words were exchanged, people said,
But they all agreed Henry Schneider
lay dead with a slug in his head.

And that small Irish tin horn gambler
known as *Johnny Behind-the-Deuce*
Held a smoking gun! "He dropped it and run!"
"A Murderer's out on the loose!

Charleston was a thriving mill town,
  Henry Schneider'd been Chief Engineer
For the Tombstone Mining and Milling firm.
  Now the miners began to appear!

There was blood in the eye of every man
  as they gathered to confer;
The throng was shouting and milling about.
  There were shouts of, "Hang the cur!"

The constable caught up with "Johnny" O'Rourke[1]
  and to save the cheap gambler's hide,
He hustled him into a wagon, they say.
  for a breakneck ten mile ride

To Tombstone, where Wyatt Earp was found
  That cold wintry afternoon
Operating his faro games
  at the Oriental Saloon.

As a dealer, Earp knew all the gamblers,
  and he certainly wasn't amused!
The bowling alley, he commandeered[2]
  to protect the endangered accused.

For every man deserves a chance—
  a chance to ride free again:
So Wyatt had said; and he put his gun
  in the place where his mouth could have been.

Then that mob of "blood lusting frontiersmen"[3]
  pursued O'Rourke into town,
They were armed and thirsting for lynching,
  and Wyatt alone faced them down.

Five-hundred to one; Earp aimed his gun
at Dick Gird, the mine's owner—what's worse,
the head of the mob! Wyatt did a good job;
Gird ordered the throng to disburse.[4]

Then Marshall Ben Sippy trundled O'Rourke
in a wagon to Tucson's big jail;
And that was the close of the wild episode—
but it seems I forgot one detail:

What became of *Johnny Behind-the-Deuce?*[5]
Did he pay the full price for his sin?
No, "Johnny" escaped from the Tucson jail
and never was heard from again.

---

1) The Constable of Charleston was George McKelvey.
2) Wyatt Earp's biographer, Stuart Lake, states that Wyatt placed O'Rourke under the guard of Morgan Earp and Doc Holliday, while Wyatt himself faced down five hundred blood-thirsty miners. *(Leo Banks, "Johnny Behind the Deuce," Days of Destiny* (Phoenix, 1996), *pp. 17-26.*
3) Lake's words.
4) Ed Schieffelin made the rich silver strike that led to the boom of the area. Assayer Richard Gird formed a partner-ship with Schieffelin, and his brother Al Gird ran the business and served as the first mayor and postmaster of Tombstone.
5) Interestingly, Editor John P. Clum in *The Tombstone Epitaph,* usually a strong Earp supporter, credits Marshall Ben Sippy alone with saving O'Rourke from the mob, with no mention of Wyatt at all.

"Buckskin Frank"

Frank Leslie gained his nickname from the buckskin shirt he persisted in wearing.

Frank Leslie put his arm about her shoulders,
As they sat upon the porch of the hotel,
Suddenly the mood was shattered,
Running footsteps loudly clattered.
Frank's romantic evening blown to hell!

Coarse epithets came ringing from the darkness,
Mike Killeen surely seemed a man deranged,
He, the husband of the woman,
All his anger now had summoned
(It mattered not the two had been estranged).

Frank met him as he thundered up the board steps
And landed on the porch, where sat his wife
With "Buckskin Frank", who never shrank;[1]
Mike must have known he gambled with his life.

He threw a punch that glanced along the shoulder
Of the buckskin-shirted man who threw a right.
'Twas a fight of brawn and muscle
As the two began to tussle,
But it soon became a different kind of fight.

Three gunshots rang out, very close together,[2]
A circle now had gathered round the two.
There was little question whether
Buckskin Frank had scarce cleared leather,
E'er they knew that Killeen's fighting days were through.

The "grieving wife," thus burdened with disaster,
Was not much pleased with playing solitaire.
For just two weeks, May Killeen tarried
Before she and Buckskin Frank were married.
(The *Epitaph* sent greetings to the pair.)

When drunk, Frank shot the flies
    from off the ceiling,
And forced his frightened wife against the wall,
Firing bullets in a swarm,
He'd outline her shapely form,
And yell, "I'm still a sure shot after all!"

Frank was said to be the finest shot in Tombstone,
He'd been, to General Crook, the chief of scouts.
Though a "Cowboy" faction backer,[3]
The Earps still hired him as tracker.
(Of his talents on the trail, there was no doubt.)

Besides bartender, prospector, rancher and scout,
Frank was known as a great story teller.
Why, he sang like a lark, wore the devil's own mark.
(Enigmatic sort of a feller!)

Old Tombstone was certainly changing,
Mike Killeen's killing would not be Frank's last.
Some say he shot Johnny Ringo;
Sure, that flashy dude gringo
Was slain by a close pistol blast!)[4]

With his pal Johnny dead, young Bill Claibourne said
He'd kill Frank for the hole in John's head,
But when they went for their guns,
Buckskin Frank clearly won:
'Twas Claibourne, "the Kid," wound up dead.[5]

Soon Buckskin's wayward eyes went back to wand'ring;
It seems that E.T. Bradshaw was found dead.
Blonde Molly'd been his woman[6]
'Fore the coroner was summoned.
(Now somebody'd shot a hole right through his head.)

Moll was one of the Bird Cage's songbirds;
When a cowhand jeered as she sang on the stage.
Buckskin heard that dumb galoot,
Shot the heel right off his boot,[7]
As the cowboy's leg was dangling from his "cage".

Now, Frank, he wooed this other *grieving widow*,
For Blonde Molly didn't seem the least bit harried.
May objected (but of course!);
She sued Buckskin for divorce.
(Frank and Molly didn't bother to get married.)

Blonde Molly moved right out to Buckskin's rancho.[8]
Not long after, whilst carousing on a spree,
Buckskin Frank shot Molly dead;
Put a slug right through her head,
Which sent Frank to Yuma penitentiary.[9]

His contributions to the famous Boot Hill graveyard,
Must have made the tombstone-cutter quite a pile.
Frank said he'd shot down three or four;
The townsfolk claimed 'twas twelve or more.
People sure knew "Buckskin Frank"
had stayed awhile![10]

Was Buckskin Frank the last jack in the card game
That was played in Tombstone's early violent years
When the town was but an angry child,
Unruly, fitful, dangerous, wild;
The last hand in the game of *Last Frontier?*[11]

---

1) Both Leslie and Killeen were employed as bartenders at the Continental Hotel saloon. Frank later went to work at the Oriental where Wyatt Earp was part owner.

2) Leslie was a ruthless man. On this occasion, Leslie, said to have been the finest marksman in Tombstone, fired two shots.

3) The "Cowboys" were the rowdy rustler gang who often shot up the town. Many of them ultimately met death at the live end of guns fired by the "Reformers," as the opposing Earp faction were called.

4) Johnny Ringo, one of the last of the "Cowboys", was found dead July 14, 1882. The newspapers reported the death as a suicide, but this was widely doubted, as his feet had been wrapped and tied with strips torn from his shirt, and his horse was found miles away with his boots tied to the saddle. There was a second wound in his forehead, presumably from a knife blade. In addition to Frank

Leslie, suspects included outlaws Billy Claibourne and Pony Deal, detective Lou Cooley, Wyatt Earp, Doc Holliday, and Michael O'Rourke (Johnny-Behind-the-Deuce).

5) Young Claibourne was called "Billy the Kid" by his cronies who compared him to the famous New Mexico outlaw.
6) Molly Williams Edwards Bradshaw. (Molly proudly added the name of each succeeding paramour: hence, now, Molly Williams Edwards Bradshaw Leslie.)
7) The suspended balcony boxes were called "cages"; hence the name "Bird Cage Theater".
8) Leslie was the caretaker on the Magnolia Ranch in the Swisshelm (Pedregosa) Mountains in southeastern Arizona.
9) On the day the he killed Molly, July 4, 1889, he also shot the young ranch foreman, "Sixgun Jimmy" Neil. Neil crawled over a mile and a half to a neighboring ranch and reported Molly's murder. For once, there was one of Frank's victims left to testify—and the jury believed him.
10) Most historians estimate that Frank Leslie had, indeed, killed about a dozen people.
11) Frank served seven years in "the city of lost hope"(Yuma Territorial Prison). A newspaper published a story and picture of Frank which led to a correspondence between him and a well-to-do divorcee named Belle Stowell. Two weeks after Frank's release in1896, he and Belle were married. Mr. and Mrs. "Buckskin" Frank Leslie vanished into the California sunset. Frank's "violent years" were about five: 1879 - 1884. Some claim he was the last of Tombstone's "bad outlaws."

From a photograph in the Southwest Studies Archives,
Maricopa Community Colleges

Wyatt Earp

Saturday Night in Tombstone

The famous "Fight at the O.K. Corral" took place four months before the first Episcopalian preacher arrived in Tombstone on January 28, 1882. Virgil Earp had served as U.S. Deputy Sheriff and U.S. Marshall. A severe bullet wound had ended his career as a lawman just a month before the incident depicted in this poem. His brother Wyatt had been appointed U.S. Deputy Sheriff for Pima (later Cochise) County. Wyatt was assisted by brother Morgan and devoted friend John Henry "Doc" Holliday.

The riders were all ridin' into Tombstone.
The well-dressed godly stranger stood amazed.
The owl-hoots were out hootin';[1]
Reckless shooters out there shootin'.
It was Saturday in Tombstone's glory days!

The hustlers were a-hustlin' on the boardwalk,
The rustlers were a musclin' into town.
Wyatt Earp durn sure was busy;
'Twas enough to make you dizzy!
Sure a good thing Doc and Morgan were around!

The place were full of miners, slicks, and cowboys,
Street walkers were a-walkin' up and down.
The hawkers were a-hawkin',
Why, the burg was fairly rockin'
The day the reverend father came to town.[2]

The gamblers were a-gamblin' at the Bird Cage;
The scramblers busy scramblin' to embark!
The boozers were a-boozin';
All the floozies, they were floozin'—
'Cause them ladies sure ain't *ladies* after dark!

The good man turned his face toward the loudest
And the wildest weirdest wicked place of sin;
The winners were a-winnin';
All the sinners were a-sinnin'
And the tin horns, they were always hornin' in.[3]

The miners were a-minin' gold at faro,
The dealers were a-dealin' tiger tight,[4]
But Wyatt wasn't able to be dealin' at his table,
Which set the Earps to urpin' there that night.[5]

The excitement was excitin' at the Bird Cage.
The footlights were all lightin' up the stage.
The reflectors were reflective;
  the effect was sure effective,
And the swingers were a-swingin' every cage.[6]

The music was a-ringin' at the Bird Cage,
The singer's song was wingin' cross the floor,
The room was dim and hazy, all crazies goin' crazy,
When that preacher set his foot inside the door.

The pi-aner man just stopped—as did the laughter.
The shoutin' and the cursin' quieten'd down.
It seemed the stroke of dooms' tone
  had just settled over Tombstone
When Endicott Peabody came to town.

He walked up to the table in the center,
And he placed his hand on Johnny Ringo's arm.[7]
The gasp was quite articulate;
  the men could scarce gesticulate,
But the outlaw didn't do the fellow harm.

"Peabody said, I'm new in your fair city, boys.
Tomorrow I'll hold service for the Lord;[8]
If you'd care to take a breather,[9]
  I'd be proud if you would be there.
By the way, we need a little cash aboard!"

Frank Leslie tossed a nugget on the table,[10]
Then Ringo threw two fifties on the board.
The pile was quickly mounting,
  why, it seemed no one was counting
The night tough Tombstone gambled for the Lord.

When criticized for taking gambled money,
Peabody said, "The sword becomes the spire!
There's no use in our recoiling;
We must keep the Lord's pot boiling,
Though we use the devil's kindling for the fire!"[11]

---

1) Owl hoots: Outlaws. What the young preacher had heard of Tombstone in Boston was that "it was the rottenest place you ever saw." (Jerry Wallace, "*How the Episcopal Church Came to Arizona, The Journal of Arizona History*", VI:3 (Autumn 1965), 111.
2) Episcopalian minister Endicott Peabody, a Cambridge graduate, established Saint Paul's, which is the oldest church in Tombstone still in use. Although Peabody may not have visited the Bird Cage on his first night in town, he was known to enter saloons, where he succeeded in persuading hard-drinking gamblers to donate to his church and charities. *Cotty*, as he was called by his friends, had been an outstanding athlete in college, and was highly respected in Tombstone, partly because he actively participated in baseball and boxing. Once he defeated the Methodist preacher and challenged and won a boxing match against a loud-mouthed tough who had threatened him.
3) Gamblers were generally respected; however, those who appeared "flashy dudes", usually itinerants who pushed their weight around, were referred to as "tin horns".
4) Playing faro was known as "bucking the tiger".
5) Wyatt was part owner of the Oriental Saloon where he operated a faro table.
6) For a considerable price, a well-heeled man could rent one of the suspended boxes, together with the *fille-de-joie* of his choice with whom to enjoy the show.
7) Johnny Ringo was one of the Clanton cattle-rustling gang called the "Cowboys". These also included "Old Man" and Ike Clanton, the McLaurys, Curly Bill Brocius, Frank Stillwell, Pony Deal and others.
8) Actually, the town's Episcopalians had not made arrangements for a service on the day following Peabody's arrival, and as there was, as yet, no church building, he conducted his first service a week later in the court room.
9) "If you'd care to take a breather": One poker game at the Bird Cage lasted nine years. When a player stopped to rest, eat, sleep or do a little rustling, he would appoint another to take his place.
10) "Buckskin Frank" Leslie had several mining claims in the Tombstone area. Many considered him the best marksman and most feared man in the county. He is said to have killed as many as a dozen men, and was one of several suspects in the shooting of Johnny Ringo six months after the evening depicted herein.

11) Parishioner Mrs. Stanley Bagg, in 1935. at age 92, quoted Peabody as saying, "The Lord's pot must be kept boiling, even if it takes the devil's kindling wood." (Henry Pickering Walker, "*Preacher in Helldorado,*" *The Journal of Arizona History*, XV: 3 [Autumn 1974], pp. 237, 248).

From a photograph in the Southwest Studies Archives,
Maricopa Community Colleges

Rev. Endicott Peabody

The Tarantula of Arizona: "Baron James Addison Peralta-Reavis"[1]

A Man of Gentility (???)

Strange stories are told of men who sought gold,
and those who found fortune and fame;
But none's more bizarre than those tales that are
related of one who came
In eighteen-hundred-and-eighty-two,
arriving in Tucson by train.

He wore a Van Dyke and surely looked like
a dandy of distinct gentility.
He told of a claim, quite sure to bring fame,
and as proof of his own credibility,
He, papers produced to serve as the proof;
yet received he but scanty civility.

Spanish land grants had not, thereto, been forgot
in this parcel acquired through the buying
Of Mexican land so U.S. could expand[2]
(Quite often such claimants were lying).

So, as one might expect, his "grant" was suspect,
seventeen thousand square miles and more, measured,[3]
Of the desert South West, including the best
of its ranch lands and mineral treasures.

This meant his domain was bigger than Maine,
Vermont and Rhode Island combined.
Phoenix, Globe, Casa Grand: (that's a whole lot of sand),
Tempe, Mesa, and more were defined.

Clifton, Safford and Florence were named in his warrants
and declared as his own territory.
As part of the land that the rascal had planned
To contribute to Reavis's glory.

So 'twas widely suspected that rents he collected
from merchants and sheep men and miners
Were illegally got by a devious plot
hatched up by a clever designer.

When they'd finished conspiring, he'd send out a hireling,[4]
who, most courteously would suggest
that the settlers pay a small fee that day
to remain on the land they possessed.

In a fortnight or so, another "agent" would go,
the same rancher or farmer to greet.
He'd demand still more dough; then the victim would show
The large and impressive receipt

Which he had received from the one who'd deceived
him by the previous claim.
"Oh, I greatly regret it's a *different* debt!"
The agent would promptly proclaim.

If rancher or miner became a decliner,
refusing to pay what he "owed,"
His horse might get shot or, likely as not,
his mine shaft was soon to explode.

To most, it seemed grievous James Addison Reavis
should enjoy such luxurious living
From lands that they'd *bought* and for which some had *fought*,
and for this they were most unforgiving.

Map #4: "The Peralta Grant"

"The Peralta Grant"

Shady Past

He was the number two son of a romance begun
 'twixt a Welsh rogue of scant credibility
And a lassie, half Scot, descended, she thought,
 from some lady of Spanish nobility.

She taught James to speak and to seek the mystique
 of the flowery Spanish romances.
She knew not, I'm afraid, the impression she made
 on a young lad of such circumstances.

In eighteen hundred and sixty one
 he signed up to fight for the gray,
Where he soon did conceive a plan to forge leaves
 for himself and those soldiers who'd pay.

He deserted three times, finally falling in line
 with the ranks of the boys in blue;
But the Feds soon got wise to his enterprise,
 so he scampered from that army too.

He was never chagrined, though he "sailed near the wind,"
 all decked out in fancy attire,
For this prince of deceit, in manner discreet,
 quite a high pile of cash had acquired.

Yes, the dishonest cad, a shady past had;
 at forgery he was the master.
Out West he began a felonious plan
 that he figured would work even faster.

To Old Mexico Reavis ventured to go,
where the curators and the librarians
All found this fine gringo, well versed in their lingo,
a veritable young antiquarian!

His Spanish descent gained him the assent
and respect of Hispanic archivists
Who allowed him to spend days and weeks upon end
'mongst cedülas, the oldest and driest.[5]

He repaid their kindness by stealing them blind, yes,
he purloined all he could conceal;
Aged parchments he'd fleece, stuff them in his valise.
Oh, he worked with unscrupulous zeal!

In the following months, he lived like a monk,
matching inks to approximation;
With his forgery skill he practiced the quill
strokes of medieval illumination.

He created a line, from two barons fine;
Oh, such impressive posterity!
Had them marrying late, so they'd not procreate
Prolific and cumbersome progeny.

Then he started to tell of the great "*Don Miguel*
de Peralta y de La Cordoba,"
Whose descent he'd devised, whose credentials comprised
"mucho mas de una *arroba*".[6]

From old Mexico to San Francisco,
where, he took up some menial pursuit
With a paper whose name could perchance bring him fame;
in this he was quite resolute.[7]

There, on mighty low pay, he finagled his way
to the railroad's high mucky mucks;
So handsome and charming, with manner disarming,
he got them investing their bucks.

From his fanciful schemes; even men with big dreams
thought Arizona the place to invest in,
So they swallowed his line, thinking things would be fine,
for their meetings were always clandestine.[8]

The First Claim: 1883

At Prescott one day, he met the roué
from whom his wild oats manifested—
Dr. Willing; to whose fame and dubious name
full many a miner attested.[9]

The Doc told the tale that a Mexican male
named *Peralta,* who'd seen better days,
Sold the old miscreant a "Spanish land grant,"
so this is what started the craze.

Still true to his creed, James quickly agreed
to a partnership with the old liar,
Toward the south he proceeded and there he succeeded
from a spark to ignite a great fire.

Still fanning the flame, Reavis filed his own claim,
and when learning that Willing was dead,
To Prescott retired, where he quickly acquired
the spurious papers, then fled.

A perceptive young clerk, who happened to work
where Reavis had filed his grand claim,
Had very grave doubts what this dude was about—
one Royal A. Johnson, his name.

Reavis bulldozed most all, the great and the small,
even Southern Pacific affected;
As they laid the new tracks, they gave him green backs
to pay for the land they dissected.

So his friends and his foes all paid through the nose,
yes, the railroad was one of his "donors."
Till his claim was disproved, he'd continue to move
by fleecing the land's rightful owners!

So smoothly he went, the U.S. Government
offered millions to make him desist
And sell out his claim; still, naught ever came
of their plan, so the scamp could persist.

The Baroness: Reavis Invents an Heiress

Reavis found a young girl, set her head in a whirl,
one of heritage quite inauspicious;
Sent her to a convent, while he himself went
to further his mission ambitious.

'Twas late one fall night, by the moon's meager light,
to Las Estrellas Montañas, he rode
There he chipped a cartouche, this sly Scaramouche,
on a prominent cliff, and bestowed

The Peralta crest he'd carved in the oak chest
that housed his spurious claim.
Then he set out to see—had nuns made a lady
of the girl he intended for fame?

He married the sweet señorita with glee,
having fully impressed and convinced her that she
Was the Peralta heir. "Absolutely!" he'd swear,
"It is chisled in stone, as you plainly can see!"[10]

"Don Miguel Nemecio Silva de
Peralta y de la Cordoba—
Your great grandfather—was the first to hold
the Barony of Arizona!

"Miguel Silva Jesus de Peralta,
now, that was your grandfather's name;
The second Baron, and you are the heir
of the Barony and its acclaim!"

'Twas surely an honor he'd bestowed upon her;
he pronounced her a lady of fame!
She, excitement suppressed, yet was greatly impressed
when she heard her new high sounding name:

Carmelita Sofia Loreta Micaela
de Maso y de Peralta,
La Baroness de Arizonac y,
tambien, de Los Colorados!

Reavis shaved off his beard, so now he appeared
wearing mutton chops long on each side;
With hair well on the way to a silvery gray;
he certainly looked dignified!

In Seville and Madrid he secretly slid[11]
his forged documents into the files,
So the seedy affair would declare her the "heir",
of the Peralta Land Grant; meanwhile,

In flea market places, he acquired the faces
to pass off as Peralta forebears:
Barons, both one and two, as well as a few
of their parents, and spouses, and heirs.

Then, he led down the aisle in true Spanish style
the heir he'd himself conjured up;
And they were soon seen by the good English Queen.
As they balanced fine china teacups.[12]

The Second Claim: 1885, Baron Peralta-Reavis

"Baron and Baroness Peralta-Reavis"
hobnobbed with the nation's high rollers
Of politics, industry, arts, and finance,
mighty magnates and moguls, controllers

Whom his ego massaged like the vast entourage
which he kept, as aristocrats greeted.
In Spain, the elite had fawned at their feet
like royalty they had been treated.[13]

So now, as the spouse of the heir to the house
of Peralta, he took his grand title,
And proclaimed for himself a part of the wealth
and the fame as his rightful requital

For all of his work, for he never did shirk
his arts of deceit from conception,
So he filed a new claim in the heiress's name,
Did the "Baron," this prince of deception!

Reavis built a stout palace where he'd hide from the malice
of those he'd extorted and fleeced.
Behind his walled yards and well-armed bodyguards
He sought his malevolent peace.

'Twas *tarantula* land, quite near Casa Grand.[14]
(If the great hairy thing's foes should find her,
The big *trap door spider* most quickly could hide her-
self, pulling her earth-door behind her.)

Likewise, to his lair, the scamp would repair
to his fortress like old Barcelona,
Thus, behind his high wall, James Reavis was called
el Tarantula del Arizona.

Thus, the redheaded rogue with his fake English brogue,
dreamed of wearing a Spanish corona,
While increasing his wealth and calling himself
the third "Baron of Arizona!"

Oh, yes! This deception had, from its inception,
been patiently, carefully planned,
Taking twenty-five years of thought, toil, and tears
by this brilliant, unscrupulous man.

The Net

The subject was sore with the smart editor
of Florence's *Enterprise;*
Long he'd tried to expose the man with fine clothes,
To Tom he held no surprise.

But Tom Weeden became a man of great fame
among the people whom Reavis extorted.
Reavis's bribes and his threats had both failed to get
young Weeden's crusading aborted.[15]

Reavis laughed, "He's a hick trying hard to be slick!
It causes me no great concern, see,
For he hasn't a prayer! He must be unaware
of all of my famous attorneys!"[16]

Surveyor General, Johnson was now;
he, too, worked for years to expose
The highhanded guy who was living so high;
in his mythical *emperor's clothes.*[17]

From a photograph in the Arizona Department of Library Archives.

James Addison Reavis, "The Baron of Arizona"

Reavis these two accused of his infamous ruse
    and openly called him a fraud.
So the slick malcontent sued the U.S. Government
    for defaming his name before God![18]

His reputation exposed and the figures disclosed —
    the millions he'd tried to extort
From the ranchers and miners and all their cosigners;
    Reavis now took his case to the courts.

In Old Santa Fe, the trial, one day
    in June, eighteen ninety-five,
Commenced—but poor James! It was really a shame—
    his attorneys all failed to arrive!

They'd all dropped him flat; when he heard about that,
    the role of a lawyer he took;
He argued and swore, as his own counselor,
    that he'd prove he was never a crook.
Yes, a shyster had dreamed an improbable scheme,
    ingenuously forming a plot,
And this *duke of deception* had from its inception,
    Meticulously tied every knot.

But 'twas finally revealed that the documents sealed
    inside his bejeweled wooden chest
Were as phony as snipe, a daguerreotype
    of the flimfiams, the cheats and the rest

Who had preceded him; yet by such pseudonym
    none before had enhanced his persona
By fictitious claim, with illustrious a name
    as el Baron del Arizona![19]

---

1) The name is sometimes written *Peraltareavis,* as it is throughout *The Baron of Arizona* by E.H. Cookridge (New York, 1967). The spelling in this poem is consistent with that in Donald M. Powell's *The "Baron of Arizona Self. Revealed, A Letter to his Lawyer in 1894." Arizona and the West, A Quarterly Journal of History,* 1:2, (Summer 1959), and most other sources consulted.
2) This was land acquired through the Gadsden Purchase, December 31, 1853. Arizona acquired the portion south of the Gila River to the present Mexican border.
3) An area two-hundred thirty-five miles long and seventy-five miles wide: "twelve million acres of land studded with gold and copper mines and with a score of. . . settlements within its boundaries. ... exceeding two thousand square miles:" (Cookridge, 21, 37). "A tract of fifty by 150 square miles in central Arizona—extending from just west of Phoenix almost to the outskirts of Silver City, New Mexico." (Powell, 161).
4) Reavis's head thug was a big mean-looking ruffian named Pedro Cuervo.
5) *Cedüla:* decree, document, certificate.
6) Mucho más de una *arroba*—well over 25 pounds.
7) The *San Francisco Examiner.*
8) This was in 1874; the *Examiner* was in dire straits, having supported the losing candidate in the recent election, as well as having harshly attacked Huntington and the Southern Pacific Railroad Syndicate. The editor was, then, utterly astonished when Reavis succeeded in selling an ad to Collis P. Huntington, one of Southern Pacific's *Big Four.* Huntington was determined to push his railroad through Arizona and New Mexico and on to New Orleans. Because Reavis assured him rights across the "Peralta Grant," Huntington, together with Charles Crocker, business manager for S.P., agreed to finance Reavis's claim.
9) "Dr." George M. Willing, Jr. was an itinerant peddler of patent medicines. Reavis claimed they met when Willing came to his office in St. Louis in 1870. (Powell, 163). Willing died at Prescott in March, 1874 of "an overdose of whiskey and laudanum—a potent mix if there ever was one." (Trimble, *In Old Arizona).* There were those who questioned the circumstances surrounding his death.
10) At the time of this marriage, December 31, 1882, Reavis was still the husband of Ada Pope, whom he'd married in May, 1874 in St. Louis. For this reason, his marriage to "the heiress" was kept secret until his divorce from Ada (for desertion) was finalized in 1883.
11) The trip to Spain was financed by Huntington and Harvey S. Brown, the company lawyer for Southern Pacific. These powerful tycoons saw, in this journey, the possibility of increasing their wealth through the strengthening of Reavis's claim. At the *Archivos de Indias* at Seville, however, Reavis was observed slipping something into one of the files. Charges were brought against him, but Reavis's highly placed friends covered for him, and he high-tailed it out of the country.

12) Carmelita had traveled to Spain as Reavis's ward, whence they were accompanied by a chaperone, French maid, and valet. They were remarried with great pomp, in the church at San Sebastian in 1886; now Reavis could openly claim the title "Baron." The English queen who invited the Reavises to tea was Victoria.

13) "The Baroness" had proved a great favorite with the aristocracy of Europe, having received audiences with the queens of both Spain and England, invitations to extravagant parties, and most elegant accommodations. She was especially admired by the gentlemen, notably the Prince of Wales and his influential male companions.

14) This was a grandiose red brick mansion, built like a fortress, which Reavis called *Arizola.* It was not far from the ancient Hohokam ruin known as the Casa Grande, which is now nearer Coolidge, (founded in 1926), than to the town of Casa Grande which was the nearest community to the ruin when that village was founded in 1880). After his return from Europe, Reavis rented a whole floor of the Fifth Avenue Hotel, where he conducted interviews with the great financiers of the nation, selling stock in a vast variety of corporations: land, roads, dams, canals, railroads, communications, precious metals, coal, livestock, farm produce, factories, mills, etc. Each of these companies bore the name Casa Grande, e.g., *Casa Grande Land and Improvement Company of Arizona, Wyoming, New Jersey,* etc. (Cookridge, 188). When things got hot, he would scurry back to Arizola, for which he was likened to the tarantula.

15) Weeden did not set out to be a champion of the people. He was simply a business man. For some time he printed Reavis's elaborate and expensive ads, but when the young editor observed the usurper's brutalizing tactics (one frightened spinster committed suicide following Reavis's threats), Weeden began his campaign for justice. Reavis first attempted to stop Weeden by bribery, as he had a Phoenix editor, then resorted to vague threats on Weeden's family. One night Weeden's office was broken into, attempts made to destroy his presses, type scattered in the road, and a fire started. (Cookridge, 114-118).

16) Reavis truly did have an array of impressive attorneys: Harvey S. Brown; company lawyer of the Southern Pacific Railroad, James O. Broadhead, President of the American Bar Association; and Robert Green Ingersoll, called "the greatest American lawyer of the nineteenth century," to whom he had been introduced by New York Senator Roscoe Conkling, leader of the Stalwart faction of the Republican party. (E. H. Cookridge, *The Baron of Arizona* [New York, 1967], pp. 49, 85, 194).

17) This was Royal A. Johnson, the clerk who had filed Reavis's first claim at Tucson. Johnson was, by this time, U.S. Surveyor General.

18) This was "the Baron's" fatal mistake, for by suing the U.S Government for eleven million dollars, he caused Federal officials to work diligently to expose him as an impostor. The case was tried at the old Territorial capitol Santa Fe, ironically, a city which was founded by a Peralta—Don Pedro, third governor of New Mexico Territory. (Cookridge, 242).

19) Although a masterpiece of criminal genius, "The Baron's" evidence was fallible. "Genuine documents had been purloined and faked to produce evidence of the Peralta Grant." (Cookridge, 208, 247-249). His errors involved "eighteenth century" copies made with nineteenth century inks; use of a steel pen not invented until 1880; authentic seals pried from aged documents and applied to Peralta papers with glue; and type, supposedly set in 1784, which was actually not available until 1885. This latter fact was brought to light by Weeden's type setter, "Stammering Bill" Truman, while Spanish language expert Severo Mallet-Prevost found technical errors in certain papers, e.g., the indicative verb form where subjunctive should have been used. The "Wisconsin watermark," said to have been found on some of the writings is, however, thought by most historians to have been fictitious. Certainly, the old fox, James Addison Reavis, was too smart to have made such an obvious mistake!

Vigilante Coming!

This incident took place in August, 1887 when Florence's Sheriff Jeremiah Fryer was out of town. The tunnel referred to in this poem was a meeting room behind the Tunnel Cafe and Tavern. It was built into a big excavation in the middle of a livery stable with a canvas nailed over the top. Pauline Cushman had been a well known actress and had won fame as a Union spy during the war between the states.

What a strange and tangled tale is told
Of what happened in Florence that night.
The air was still, unmercifully hot,
The streets bathed in brilliant moonlight.

The sheriff and under sheriff, it seems,
Had been called out of town for awhile.
Jailer Rice and County Attorney Sloan[1]
Were sleeping outside of the jail.

'Round twelve o'clock they were shaken awake,
By a guy who did odd jobs 'round town.
He said, "There's a mob in the tunnel tonight,
And word has been goin' around

"That they're plannin' to take your prisoners,
String 'em up from a cottonwood tree.
They say since there's only two of you here,
It ought to be simple, you see."

Imprisoned were four declared killers
That Mike Rice was bound to protect,
But first he must make pretty certain,
Since his source was slightly suspect.

So he slipped along a back alley
To the canopied tunnel and heard
The plan that the men were discussing:
Just as he'd been told—word for word.

Now Rice knew a gunfighter-killer
Who ran a saloon in the town,
And Mike Rice himself had witnessed
Him shooting an unarmed man down.[2]

Dave Gibson had been acquitted
In Tucson a few years before,
And, desperate for armed assistance,
The jailer walked through the bar's door.

Now, Gibson agreed to assist him
And posted a sign *Bar Closed.*
Surely more unlikely partners
Had seldom been seen than those!

These two, plus himself, the attorney Sloan,
Plus four others, he planned to arm.
A desperate plan! Could just seven men
Keep the interred suspects from harm?

But Richard Sloan, refused to assist
In Rice's absurd little plan.[3]
So hurrying down to the sheriff's house,
And lacking another good man,

Rice wakened the sheriff's beautiful wife,
Pauline Cushman, of Late-Great War fame,
Who was as well known for marksmanship
As her acting and spying could claim.

She hurriedly dressed and armed herself
With a Winchester rifle, and she,
When seated alone at the sheriff's desk,
Appeared just as calm as could be.

Then, Rice went to the cells of his prisoners
And explaining the plan he'd devised,
He charged each man on his honor to stand,
And help him to save their own lives.

He would give all four of them rifles
Which would help fortify the small jail;
They would seem to be four good deputies
And if his shrewd plan didn't fail,

They would fool the enraged vigilantes,
But when the fierce mob was quelled,
They must agree to give up the weapons
And return once more to their cells.

They agreed, and he took them all upstairs—
Brash, Emerson, Dozier, and Dunn—
To the court room on the floor above;[4]
There they waited until they'd begun

To hear the sound of tramping feet
As the mob approached for assault.
Then Rice stuck his head out the window
And ordered the marchers to halt.

"I've got four well-armed deputies with me—
And more in the office below!"[5]
Barrels of Winchester rifles appeared;
The advancing vanguard was slowed.

"You come at your peril, you blood-thirsty skunks!
And some of you soon will be dead
If you take just one more step forward," he yelled,
"We'll fill you all plumb full of lead!"

The effect was shock! That resolute flock
Scattered just like a covey of quail.
Rice, turning anew to his motley crew,
Hoped the rest of his scheme wouldn't fail!

For there he sat till the August dawn
In that courtroom with four well armed men—
His erstwhile *prisoners*—and wondered, did he,
Just which thought was going to win:

The temptation to gain their *freedom*
Or their forsworn *honor* and *word.*
The one he feared most was Emerson:
Rough drifter, tough, hard-bitten bird.

Dozier and Dunn were neighborhood boys,
Young; had no offenses before,
They'd been hired by Brash to kill Joe White
In some local water rights war.

Rice told them all to give up their guns
And go peaceably back to their cells.
The two younger boys did just as he said,
But Brash didn't settle so well.

Then Emerson, placing his rifle
To the side of Brash's big head,
Just herded him back to the cell block,
Locked him in, and quietly, said,

"Come on, Mike, and get these two rifles,
I'm layin' 'em here on the floor.
You've treated us fair and I'm true to my word!"
And he closed and locked his cell door.

And what happened when the sheriff returned?
Some folks thought that Mike Rice should be fired.
"The prisoners are safe in their cells." He shrugged.
That's the purpose for which I was hired!"

---

1) Richard Elihu Sloan was Pinal County Attorney from 1887 to 1889. He later became Justice of Arizona Supreme Court and the last territorial governor. (John S. Goff, *Arizona Biographical Dictionary*, 1983; p. 91).

2) Gibson and three cohorts had gunned down "the Pioche Gunfighter" Jim Levy (James Dunlevy) as he emerged unarmed from the Palace Saloon in Tucson.

3) Historians differ on Sloan's action here. For example, *Charles D. Lauer (Tales of Arizona Territory)* states that Sloan assisted Rice. In a personal letter to this author, however, John A. Swearingin, author of *Good Men, Bad Men, Law Men* and long-time Florence resident, contends: "When I returned to the jail," Rice said, "I found the District Attorney's cot had vanished and it's owner, like a gopher chased by a cat, crawled into his hole and tarantula like, pulled the hole after him."

4) Swearingin also disagrees with Lauer in stating that there was only one floor to the Florence jail.

5) Gibson was actually stationed in an abandoned adobe house across the alley from the jail.

From a photograph in the Library of Congress Archives, Washington, D.C.

Pauline Cushman

The Rhyming Robber

W.R. "Red" McNeil came to Holbrook in 1887 at the age of 20.

McNeil was called "Red the Rooster",
James, Wallace, or Howe, or King.[1]
He was friendly, cheerful, handsome;
He could do most anything!

Didn't say just where he'd come from
With his clothes rolled in a tarp,
But he sang old songs and told good tales,
And danced as he played the mouth harp!

Some said he had come from Boston;
Others said from Vermont or Maine,
But he seemed plumb educated,
And his language confirmed the same.

He joined us up west of Holbrook,
Had a grin that wouldn't quit.
Boss hired him on as a rider
For that Aztec cow outfit

Which was often called the Hash Knife
For that controversial brand.[2]
Tons of tough old Texas longhorns
And a million square of land.

Now, Red was a fine bulldogger.
He could shoot right straight and true;
Good roper, and what a twister!
He's one hell of a buckaroo![3]

The mercantile, A. and B. Schuster's,
Was robbed late one evening in May.
Ben fired at the redheaded robber;
Adolf saw the guy run away.

Whilst fixing breakfast, our cookie
Watched Red picking buckshot 'fore dawn,
By daybreak the kid was missing—
And four of our best horses gone.

Left a note for the brothers Schuster;
"I'm still carrying your lead,
But if you would kill this rooster,
Got to shoot him in the head!"[4]

We learned he was wanted in Phoenix
For "borrowing" somebody's horse;
And that he'd broke jail down at Florence,
So he's wanted there too, of course.

Turned up in New Mexico shortly;
At the French Ranch he stopped for awhile.
Will French thought him just a chuck liner,
But he liked the young cowpuncher's style.[5]

Red said he'd worked for the Hash Knife,
And rather than wait for his pay,
He'd taken his salary in horseflesh—
"Los caballos bonitos!" he'd say.

He sang and he danced for the waddies;
He stayed there well over a week.
Then Will found his Thoroughbred missing:
The stallion he'd named *Pow-a-Sheik.*

They trailed the daring young outlaw.
Wanted! posters French posted about
New Mexico and Arizona—
And Old Mexico too, I've no doubt.

Then an envelope postmarked *Clifton*
Brought an altered poster which read
That "Due to a horse theft near Alma,"
Will French was now wanted by Red![6]

Old French was plumb flabbergasted;
Yet, he had to smile at the cheek
Of the rascally redheaded robber
Who'd stolen his fabulous Sheik.

Sheriff Commodore Perry Owens,
With his long hair and cross-holstered guns,
Was growing tired of waiting
While young Rooster Red had his fun.[7]

Owens vowed he'd catch that robber—
Said there wasn't any doubt!
He commenced interrogating
All the cow camps round about.

He rode up on a small outfit
That the Waters family ran
And commenced inquiring of them—
Had they seen the young wanted man?

The evening was damp and chilly;
One, seeing the poor lawman's plight,
Said, "Sheriff, come share my bedroll;
Its mighty dang cold out tonight!"

Awakening in the morning,
The sheriff, at first light of dawn,
Observed that the camp was empty—
Every horse and cowboy was gone.

A note had been pinned to the blanket;
Said the thief who had robbed Schuster's store
Was his bed-mate as well as the horse thief
That the sheriff was out looking for!

The *Herald* from over at St. Johns
Printed a verse that it had received;
To all of Red's earlier victims
Plus the sheriff whom he'd just deceived:

"I am the prince of the Aztec!
I'm perfection at robbing a store.
I've a stake left me by Wells Fargo;
Before long I'll have even more!

"A few words to all of my friends, now—[8]
And I certainly have quite a few—
Though we be at daggers' ends now,
I still send a Howdy-you-do!

"The sheriff is wanting to kill me;
That sounds like a whole lot of fun!
'Tis strange that he hankers to drill me,
This redheaded sun of a gun.

"He handles a six-shooter neatly;
Gets a rabbit at nigh every pop.
Should the sheriff and I chance to meet up,
We'll have us an Arkansas hop!"

Coconino County lawmen
Were confounded by young Red too;
They tracked him to Clear Creek Canyon
But, incredibly, he slipped through.

Although surrounded by posse,
And volleys of shots were exchanged,
They found a note in a cabin,
In which he, quite briefly, explained:

"Perhaps you all are now wondering
At the fiery reception you got;
In-as-much as it is my birthday,
A pyrotechnical show, I thought

Appropriate to the occasion
With a welcoming greeting to boot;
For its seldom I'm favored with guests here;
Thus, the special Winchester salute!"

Red was seen once more in Holbrook,
Stole a horse and wrote to the press.
Rode north cross the reservation;
And the Holbrook paper professed:

"There's something to be admired in
Such dare-devil recklessness.
He's never shed another's blood
And his humor can't be suppressed."

Robbed a train in Colorado—
(Called Fisher or Dayton by then);
Then he, for a heist pulled at Ogden,
Wound up in the Utah State Pen.

They said that all he had asked to keep,
While up there serving his time,
Was that little old dented mouth harp.
Why, it couldn't have cost more'n a dime!

Will French lost track of the outlaw,
But 'twas said that quite often he'd speak
Of the charming disarming bandit
Who stole his Arabian Sheik:

French said, "Don't know where he is now,
But I'm sure if he served up his time,
He came out a-blowin' that mouth harp
Or spoutin' some dang silly rhyme

And dancin', a double shuffle
On the pavement, that cockatiel!
That rascally redheaded rooster,
That rhyming rogue, Red McNeil!

Epilogue

Thirty years later in Holbrook,
A stranger stepped down from the train.
Wore a fine cravat and derby
And walked with a horse-headed cane.

This "professional looking stranger"
Showed up at the old Schuster store.
"Former resident of Holbrook," he said,
And he was inquiring for

The merchant brothers Schuster;
Sorry to hear Ben passed away,
But he talked awhile with Adolf,
And later showed up in L.A.

Where the old man moved thereafter;
And there, like a good creditor,
He paid Adolf Schuster the money
Stolen thirty-five years before.

---

1) Red had many aliases.
2) Brand in shape of the meat chopper, similar to a Rocker T.
3) *Twister:* bronc buster.
Buckaroo: cowboy. Said to have been the preferred term of the cowboys themselves.
4) McNeil must have known of the 1870s exploits of California's gentleman robber *Black Bart* (Charles E. Bolton), who left rhymes at the site of his robberies. Some of Red's verses have been slightly edited for meter. I am sure he could have done as well himself but, after all, he was often pressed for time.
5) The William French Ranch was near Alma, NM. A *chuck (or grub) line rider* was a cowboy who moved from place to place, hoping for a few free meals or for short term employment.
6) Red had, of course, done this cut and paste job himself.
7) Navajo and Apache Counties were not separated until 1895. In Red's time, Commodore Perry Owens was sheriff of Apache County.
8) Red poetically referred to his victims as "my friends".

Red the Rooster

Young Red was a cowhand who uster
    rob stores like the A. and B. Schuster,
But their shot flew so hot
    that he wished he had not,
For now he's a true buckarooster!

The Hangin' Tree

The incident on which this poem is based took place August 11, 1888 in what was then known as Apache (now Navajo) County, Arizona. The hanging is often considered part of the Pleasant Valley War.

More heinous traitors ne'er defiled
a host's wide open door,
Since those were housed at Glencoe
nigh two hundred years before.[1]

There's a pine that stands high on the rim
of the mighty Mogollon,
Above where Canyon and Tonto Creeks
sing in cheerless tuneless tones.
Gold light glints on the needles,
as an east wind starts to blow,
As it did one summer morning
past a hundred years ago

When a lawless mob of twenty-eight,
in one collective breath,
Sent three young and hardy cowboys
to a rude untimely death.
James Stott, Jim Scott, Jeff Wilson[2]
were the hapless punchers three
Who swung that fatal morning
from the branch of the hangin' tree. [3]

The mob claimed to have a warrant—
though they couldn't produce the proof,
And Jamie fixed them breakfast,
and they ate beneath his roof.
It was known he kept a record
of all the stock he got—
What he bought and sold and traded,
did young rancher, Jamie Stott.
(Some claimed he listed what he stole
as well as what he bought).

Now, they might have called him "Easterner",
   or "that dude that went to school";
Some dared to call him "horse thief,"
   but none could call him fool!
And what could be more foolish
   in the law's discerning eyes
Than to leave a tidy record
   that could mean one's own demise?

Most declared the claims unfounded,
   said some coveted the land
That the young cowboy had settled—
   high clean mountain meadows and
Abundant rushing waters,
   rich green grasses growing high
Enough to touch a horse's belly
   as a man went riding by.

Now it never has been proven
   if they were innocent or not,
But Jeff, called "the unknown cowboy",[4]
   Jimmy Scott and Jamie Stott,
If guilty of the several crimes
   those men claimed that they had done,
Were still killed by craven cowards—
   odds were nearly ten to one.

Though Jeff and Jim died quickly,
   jerked from backs of bolting steeds,
Jamie Stott was cruelly tortured
   and tormented, for indeed,
Some of the mob themselves were sickened
   by the treatment of young Stott,
And they whispered the tale long after
   of how valiantly he fought.

Several said the one reputed
to be leader of the band
Had bragged his sheep would some day graze
on Jamie's fertile land;
And Jamie's grieving father,
the remainder of his days,
Knew those sheep were grazing peacefully
o'er Jamie's nameless grave.[5]

Still, the heart within the living trunk
of the hangin' tree weeps away;
And the aspens, trembling, whisper
about what transpired that day.

---

1) A reference to the February, 1692 "Massacre of Glencoe" in Scotland, wherein the MacDonalds of Glencoe were murdered in their beds by government troops, whom they had sheltered from a blizzard for more than two weeks.
2) Jeff Wilson was also known as Billy Wilson.
3) The most controversial of the three young men was 24-year-old James W. Stott, son of a prosperous Massachusetts woolen mill executive. Jamie, as young Stott was called, had come to Arizona expecting to work for the Aztec Land and Cattle Company. This arrangement fell through, so Jamie went into business for himself. This handsome, personable young man was well liked by some and highly resented by others.
4) Leland J. Hanchett, Jr., *The Crooked Trail to Holbrook* (Phoenix, 1993), p. 88.
5) The graves are now marked by small concrete headstones indicating the name and dates of birth and death of each young man, but these were placed many years after the hangings. In his book *The Crooked Trail to Holbrook,* Leland J. Hanchett, Jr. contends that the date thereon is incorrect, that the hangings actually took place August 11, 1888 rather than August 4, as the markers indicate. Several years after Jamie's death, his father had a monument erected for him in the Lowell, MA cemetery.

From photographs by J. C. Burge, "Artistic Photographer," Flagstaff, Arizona. Courtesy of the Arizona Historical Society.

Jamie Stott and Jeff (Billy) Wilson

"Climax Jim: My Favorite Outlaw"

When Rufus Nephew, alias Jim Thomas, worked on the Hash Knife spread, his penchant for Climax chewing tobacco caused the boys to dub him "Climax Jim". He became one of the most notorious cattle rustlers and elusive prisoners in northern Arizona Territory in the 1890s. In 1901 Arizona reporter George H. Smalley wrote an article for San Francisco Examiner *entitled "Climax Jim: My Favorite Outlaw".*

Jim entered the cattle business.
With a ranch he was not encumbered.
He rustled all of his stock, they say,
his total take was unnumbered.[1]

Now, Jim was so good with a running iron,[2]
it seemed no brand could dissuade him;
So no one could prove he broke the law,
and no jail could blockade him.

"Most slippery bird in the whole southwest,"
said the Solomonville newspaper.[3]
Of all the slipperies, Jim was best
Arizona's top escaper!

At picking locks, Jim surely was
the undisputed master.
Were there a test, he'd have proved the best
and would have done it faster!

For Jim, ropes, chains, bolts, latches, and bars
Held no intimidation;
He picked handcuffs, leg irons, key style locks,
and those with combinations.

There was the time in St. Johns jail,
Jim ranted while undressing,
Clouted the lawman with his pants
and ran. He kept them guessing![4]

He crawled into a camp that night,
his boots he'd left behind him,
Now, horseless, shoeless, hapless too:
the guy who chanced to find him

Felt mighty happy that cold night,
  to help the unlucky stranger,
For the man into whose camp he'd crawled
  was an Arizona Ranger![5]

In that secluded mountain camp
  Jim, claiming to be chilly,
Threw so much brush upon the fire
  he made the law look silly;

Suddenly blinded by thick smoke
  and sparks from glowing embers,
The choking ranger wiped his tears,
  as his horse—and Jim—hit timbers.

Then another sheriff captured Jim,
  and they, handcuffed together,
Undignified, lay side by side,
  in cold, inclement weather.

And when the sheriff woke at dawn,
  head propped on saddle leather,
He found his horse and Jim were gone,
  and his own wrists cuffed together.

When back at his job as "cattle boss,"
  a wide loop Jim would swing,
Then, due to his art with a running iron,
  no one could prove a thing!

He sold a dozen stolen steers
  to the mine company butcher shop
at Clifton, then altered the payment check
  so that he would come out on top.

As the law couldn't prove he was rustling,
  they arrested him for check kiting,
And the prosecution produced the note;
  so what was the use of Jim fighting?

Pronouncing the check as "Exhibit A",
  the voice of the prosecution
Said, "Climax can't escape this time!
  He must face his retribution!"

To his attorney Jim whispered, "Object!"
The young lawyer loudly objected!
The two counsels clashed vociferously;
the defendant seemed quite unaffected.

In all the commotion, Jim took a chew
and no one so much as eyed him,
Nor saw him lay the wet plug down
on the table there beside him—

On top of foresaid, "Exhibit A",
the check placed there for viewing.
"Order!" The judge's gavel fell,
as Jim sat calmly chewing.

Jim spat his wad in the handy spittoon,
and nobody saw what followed.
It seems he took a second chaw;
and no one noticed—he swallowed.

The check and the plaintiff's case were gone,
and for this incompetence,
The judge pronounced the case dismissed
—for lack of evidence.

---

1) "How many Indian ponies and herds of cattle he drove out of Arizona and sold in New Mexico will never be known." (Spoken by Ranger Joe Pearce in Smalley's "*Climax Jim, My Favorite Outlaw,*" *Arizona Highways*, April 1949).
2) Running iron—A plain branding iron used by rustlers for changing brands.
3) The *Solomonville Bulletin*. (Leo Banks, *Rattlesnake Blues*, [Phoenix, 2000], p. 108). Solomonville (later Solomon), is in Graham County.
4) Feigning a temper tantrum, Jim threw his boots and shirt around his open-doored cell. Deputies refused to pay any attention. One dozed in his chair. Jim took off his trousers, rushed from his cell and hit the other deputy in the face with them, then dashed out into the darkness, carrying his pants.
5) This was Ranger Joe Pearce. Pearce, not having learned of the St.Johns jail break, arrested Jim for attempting to steal his horse.

From a photograph in the Arizona Department of Library Archives.

"Climax Jim: My Favorite Outlaw"

The Blundering Bungling Bandits[1]

'Twas on January the thirtieth
  in eighteen ninety five,
The S.P. train had slowed to make
  the grade that's just outside
Of Willcox, when the engineer
  to his uttermost surprise,
Felt cold hard steel against his head,
  as a voice like steel advised
He stop at the crest—with which request,
  he readily complied.
Jolts and jars of uncoupling cars
  proved his fears were justified.

"Drive forward now, till I yell 'Stop!'"
  the hard cold voice commanded;
So this he did, well knowing that
  his passengers were stranded.
With the engine and express car,
  the robbers intended to stay
Well ahead of the rest, pursuing their quest
  for a clean fast get-away.
In Willcox they'd bought dynamite,
  and lest anyone be suspecting,
Had stated loud around the town:
  "We'll soon be off *prospecting*!"

Five miles west of Willcox,
  they'd stashed it in a gorge,
Had these nervous novice bandits,
  Grant Wheeler and Joe George.
As the train slowed on the rising grade,
  they jumped on and began,
By dealing thus with the engineer,
  to carry out their plan:
Around the two great iron safes,[2]
  the pair stuck dynamite,
Lit the fuse and ran like hell,
  then observed the strangest sight!

The deafening explosion
    of the small safe burst the door,
Revealing "*dobe dollars*"! [3]
    Yet, as strong as it was before,
The other safe stood staunchly,
    and the robbers cursed their fate.
They must crack the big Wells Fargo,
    before it was too late!
They used the sacks of pesos, then,
    as ballast for the job;
They piled them high atop the safe
    they had resolved to rob.

They set a charge of powder—
    enough to destroy the train;
And thousands of *dobe dollars*,
    just like wind-driven rain
Blown by a great tornado,
    spewed over the barren plain.
When smoke had cleared, the bandits
    searched all that was left of the car.
They found that what was in that safe,
    it's sturdy door ajar,
Was nothing compared to the wasted wealth
    lying scattered near and far—

A fortune in Mexican silver!
    A few handfuls which they grabbed
Before riding right into the night
    for fear of being nabbed.
(For years the people of Willcox,
    remembering that night,
Would rake around that desert ground
    for the loot that had taken flight.)
The whole endeavor was a flop,
    the boys had had their fun,
But instead of ending their crime career,
    it was only chapter one!

So what about those intrepid two?
Chagrined that they had failed,
They vowed that they'd try the plan again,
that success might yet prevail!
Again they jumped aboard the cab
Not far from Doubtful Canyon,
Where the same engineer and fireman,
They found as their companions.
Wheeler said, somewhat sheepishly,
"Well, here we are again!"[4]
His laugh seemed somewhat nervous,
for they'd boarded the self same train!

George held the fireman and engineer
at bay with his trusty Colt,
While Wheeler left to uncouple cars.
Then came that familiar jolt!
When he reappeared, the engineer
was advised to pour on the steam,
Leaving the passenger cars behind,
to complete the same old scheme;
But when the engine reached the place
where they'd left their dynamite,
They realized an awful fact;
Wheeler's one slight oversight:

"Now we're ready to blow the safes!"
The bandits then concluded.
The other cars were all unhitched—
the *express car* not excluded—
"Where's the car where the safes are kept?"
Ah, pity the bandits' plight!
They sent the engine back along the track
and they blew up their dynamite![5]

---

1) The title is derived from Marshall Trimble's "*Bungled Burglaries,*" from which most of the information in the poem is derived. (*In Old Arizona,* [Phoenix 1993], pp. 47-49). To this author, Trimble stated, "This story has more kinks than a cheap lariat," but he has been most helpful in assisting to track down the most likely particulars.

2) In his book named for this event, (*Shot in the Ass With Pesos, A Collection of Frontier Tales [Tucson 1979], p. 7*). "Budge" Ruffner mentions only "the little express company safe."

3) *Dobe dollars:* - Mexican Pesos.

4) The second attempt was only a few weeks later, in February, 1896.
5) Trimble contends that both of the robbers were eventually hanged. *(In Old Arizona,* p. 49). Ruffner claims that Grant Wheeler took his own life near Mancos, Colorado, as a posse was closing in on him, but advises, "If you ever see an old man with a few silver pesos pasted to his posterior, call the sheriff of Cochise County." *(Shot in the Ass,* p. 7).

From a photograph in the Southwest Studies Archives, Maricopa Community Colleges.

Grant Wheeler

III. Just Plain Folks: 19th Century

"A homely hero, born of star and sod;
a Peasant-Prince, a Masterpiece of God."

— Walter Malone

"The humblest citizen of all the land, when clad in the armor of a righteous cause, is stronger than all the hosts of error."

— William Jennings Bryan

Torch Light Christmas Eve

Setting: Northern Arizona.
Time: December, 1853.
Cast: Army Corps of Topographical Engineers seeking railroad routes across the Southwest.

At the foot of San Francisco Peaks
one bleak December day,
A group of weary travelers made their camp.
Their chief, Lieutenant Whipple,
who had led them all the way,
could see the men were tired, cold and damp. [1]

Tomorrow would be Christmas Eve,
but there wasn't any cheer;
Dark clouds all seemed to forecast still more snow,
And this bunch of hungry, grumpy
topographic engineers
knew they still had quite a long hard way to go.

While the cook was fixing supper,
the Lieutenant found a keg
Containing several gallons of good hooch, [2]
Then a great big iron kettle
and a crate of chicken eggs.
He knew exactly what he had to do!

He started mixing eggnog
by his special recipe
The eggs, the liquor, something from his pack—
A vial containing fluid
(maybe liquid dynamite
kept for unexpected alien attacks!)

The next evening, cold and cloudy,
    all the boys were milling round.
Cook, he hollered, "Come and get it!" and they did.
Though they'd shoveled one big circle,
    snow was slushy on the ground.
    they ate standing by the fire, like great big kids.

But the mood had changed for better,
    Christmas food especially good,
Then Whipple filled tin cups with bubbling brew.
They kept coming back for refills,
    it was like some miracle
    was mixed up in that pot of Christmas dew.

Then they sat around the camp fire
    on old boxes, kegs and stools,
Smoked, drank toasts, told stories, poems, riddles, jokes.
Two fiddles and a cornet
    quite suddenly appeared
    and a sergeant started dancing in the smoke.

The assistants commenced singing
    drinking songs of Mexico,
And everybody tried to sing along.
Then two, who had been captives
    of a group of Navajos,
    did Indian dances. Cookie beat the gong.

Two privates snatched up fire brands;
    it became a wild affair—
A whooping, leaping, laughing Christmas choir
Who sang in seven languages,
    but no one seemed to care;
    then someone set a tall lone pine afire.[3]

The heat caused the high branches
  to dump great clumps of snow
Which set the bunch to howling even louder;
Two or three more pines were lighted,
  their tops like candles glowed.
  must have heated up the clouds—they sifted powder.

Antoine Leroux sat watching this Bacchanalian revelry
"Great way to signal Indians!" scoffed the scout[4]
But, at last, the men were sleeping,
  didn't wake for reveille,
  (for the bugler didn't wake, himself, no doubt).

Their artist, in his journal,
  wrote that Christmas Day was spent
"In perfect silence," (no one wondered why),
"To honor our creator, we'd but to look at the sublime
  snow clad summits of those Peaks against the sky."[5]

---

1) The San Francisco Peaks (or Mountains) were named by Franciscan monks at Oraibe in 1629 to honor their patron saint, Francis of Assisi. The officer in charge was Lieutenant Amiel Whipple. (Barnes, p. 85 and Trimble, *Arizoniana* [1988, Scottsdale], pp. 75-76).

2) Actually, it was Lieutenant John Jones, rather than Whipple, who discovered the cache of rum and wine.

3) "When darkness came on Christmas Eve, the camp was a merry scene. In the light of the roaring campfires, Americans and Europeans sang their traditional Christmas songs, and the Mexicans enacted their customary religious plays. Leroux's Crow Indian servant and a Mexican herder began singing an improvised ballad in which they took the liberty of saying what they pleased about various individuals present. For noise, The Mexicans fired the surplus gunpowder which Whipple had given them." (David E. Conrad. *"The Whipple Expedition in Arizona," Arizona and the West,* XI:2 [Summer, 1969], p. 163).

4) Leroux was the highly respected guide who had led the Mormon Battalion from Santa Fe to California in 1846 and was the guide on three of the four Topographical Expeditions for railroad routes. A spring at the foot of San Francisco Peaks, as well as a street in Flagstaff, have been named for him.

5) German artist and naturalist, Baldwin Möllausen, was included in the expedition to depict the natural phenomena of the area. What Baldwin actually said was, "We looked up at the sublime summits of the San Francisco Mountains and needed no temple made with hands wherein to worship our creator." (Trimble, *Arizoniana*, p. 76).

From a photograph in Oklahoma Historical Society Archives.

Lt. Amiel Whipple

Shadows

After the California gold rush of 1849 had proven fruitless for most, thousands of depressed miners started the eastward trek for home. Both going and coming, many passed through New Mexico Territory, of which Arizona was then a part. Some stayed to try their luck in this new area. By the end of the Civil War, Arizona was a territory unto itself. "Go West, young man!" seemed the only answer for many a defeated, discouraged, and disillusioned Confederate soldier.

It's a mighty hopeless feelin'
when your side has lost the war;
And your home is gone, and no one's needin'
Rebel soldiers anymore.

I come out West. It wasn't
any longin' to be free
Or chasin' idle rainbows—
it was pure necessity.

I thought I'd ride as pointer,[1]
but I cough and choke and gag
And recall the smoke of battle,
as I'm spittin' dust on drag.

I look out acrost the prairies,
and I try to stop the war
That keeps ragin' on inside me,
just as vi'lent as before.

Thinkin' 'bout them poor dirt farm boys
dyin' in the fields to save
The right of some damn wealthy planter
to grow richer ownin' slaves.

Now I've figured out for certain
that the ones that start the war
Ain't the ones that do the dyin'—
and they ain't worth dyin' for;

And it actually don't matter,
    in the chilly light of dawn,
If you're out there dead or dyin',
    which side you'uz fightin' on.

I lost two brothers and an uncle,
    friends and cousins in that war;
And it really makes me wonder
    what the hell we'uz fightin' for.

Because squattin' by this campfire,
    my best buddies, Slim and Jake—
One's a darky—t'other's Yankee—
    they'd risk hell for my damn sake.

And I fight as hard beside 'em,
    battlin' cows in wild stampede
As I used to fight ag'in' 'em—
    just 'cause someone said I needed

To despise 'em,
    told me they was cruel and wrong,
And that God would bring *us* victory—
    so we'd raise our triumph song!

But when Yankees asked for victory—
    why, the same pale stars would shine
And the God that *they* was prayin' to—
    was just the same as mine.

Well, it seems a mite peculiar,
    but I've observed of late,
That the people I like, mostly,
    are the ones I'uz taught to hate.

Now I find that damn amusin',
    and I affirm it once again—
As I watch Jake drinkin' coffee
    or I see Slim's toothless grin.

God! I jolt up from a nightmare
 of my captain screamin' "Fire!"
We was back at old Fort Wagner[2]
 stumblin' through the blood and mire.

Ugh! I wake up in a clammy sweat,
 and yet I have to grin
A-rollin' in my blanket
 that the sticks is stickin' in.

For my buddies here beside me,
 knockin' rocks from 'neath their backs—
damned if one ain't a Damn Yankee!—[3]
 and the other one ain't black!

---

1) Pointer: The point riders were the two who rode in front of the trail herd to keep it properly directed.
2) Fort Wagner, South Carolina. This was only the fourth battle in which former slaves, long eager to fight, had been officially allowed to do so in the Union Army. It was fought from July 18 - September 7, 1863. The speaker in this poem had actually fought under Gen. P. G. T. Beauregard against black Yankee soldiers of the 54th Massachusetts Infantry, commanded by Col. Robert Gould Shaw who was killed. This was a siege operation against the fort, which resulted in fierce hand-to-hand fighting before the Federals were routed. Estimated casualties: 1,689 (US=1,515; CSA=174).
3) The term "damn yankee" was so commonplace, that many children grew up in the south believing it was all one word.

"I watch Jake drinkin' coffee . . ."

Big Babe's Nightcap

This incident probably occurred in the late 1860s.

Till Phoenix constructed an official hoosegow,
slight offenders were chained to a log,
Into which iron staples were driven, until
the culprit was out of his fog.

One night a big fellow who's known as "Babe" Dove
was arrested for "drunken disorder",
This wasn't the first time; this bruiser had been
the small town's most frequent night boarder.

Till midnight Babe sat on the log, deep in thought,
but his throat just kept getting drier,
And when he simply could stand it no more,
his one overwhelming desire

Drove him to shoulder the huge prison log,
and though it was certainly risky,
To the tavern across the way, he strolled
and demanded a big shot of whiskey.

The bartender was astonished, that's sure,
And poured Babe a couple of drinks;
Then, hauling the log back where it belonged,
Babe lay down and fell fast asleep.

Pájaro

(Pá-ha-ro: Bird)

In the summer of eighteen seventy six
into Florence three Mexicans rode.
Their horses all showed the effects of the miles
from Chihuahua with pretty good load.
They headed right straight for the local corrals,
and there they engaged in discourses,
Instructing the boy to feed good grain and hay
and to take good care of their horses.

"Porque," they said, they'd a long trip ahead,
so their mounts and their burdened pack beasts
Must be up to the test, so they'd take a short rest,
and then they'd be heading *northeast.*
They were seen for a week round the local saloons,
where they gambled at poker and faro.
They were jovial and friendly, and, people observed,
seemed pretty well stocked with dinero.[1]

And when well acquainted, the tall one inquired:
Would the locals enjoy a horse race?
It might just be fun, and they'd select one
of their own from the stable, in that case.
The townspeople, happy to find an excuse
to whip up a little excitement,
Accepting the challenge, agreed to a race.
(They had only needed incitement.)

Now this is what the strangers proposed:
their horse against any three
Of Florence's finest fleet-footed steeds.
Here's what the procedure would be:
The event would consist of a nine mile race,
each American horse would run three.
(Imagine one of those Mexican plugs
against three of the best in this country!)

The Mexican cayuse[2] would go all nine miles;
his American opposition
Would switch his own saddle to each relay horse;
Now these were the strangers' conditions.
The locals inspected the three sorry nags
the strangers had ridden to Florence.
None of them held a flicker of light
to the best of our own native horses.

Lou Bailey put up his gelding, the black.
Jim Sam owned the Chinese cafe,
And he'd wager his restaurant, his cattle and cash
on the speed of his big dapple gray.
Pete Gabriel offered his fast sorrel mare.
Race these fine horses? How funny!
But the Mexicans started collecting the bets:
ten to five, ten to six, even money.[3]

And then they proceeded to ready their choice:
a nondescript dunny *pack horse*
Which they called Pájaro (strange, don't you think?),
but they all set to working full force.
They combed all the cockle-burrs out of his tail,
worked the fallen hair out of his hide,
They curried and exercised, washed and massaged;
then the small one prepared for the ride.

And all of the while the news spread across
the length of the territory;
Ranchers arriving in Florence each day
with horses and cattle and money
To bet against those Mexican boys
and their pitiful pack horse Pájaro.
"That one's for the birds!" the miners all laughed,
as they laid down their bets. (¡Incrédulo!)[4]

The day of the race dawned cloudless and fair.
The first heat started in style.
The gray led Pájaro barely a length
at the end of the first three miles.
The American rider leapt from the gray,
jerked his saddle; and onto the back
Of Lou Bailey's gelding, he cinched it and rode,
leaning forward, astride the sleek black.

But Pájaro led by an eighth of a mile
  when the gelding slid in to a halt.
Fast the saddle was switched to Gabriel's mare.
  Now, was it that fine sorrel's fault
That Pájaro, flying, finished the race—
  all nine miles—and a quarter to good?
The Mexican fellows collected their loot,
  just as they had known that they would.

We watched the three winners
  prepare to leave town.
  the small one, the tall one, the fat one.
They left as they came, their mounts were the same;
  and Pájaro? Who'd notice that one?
These boys were not fools! For loaded like mules
  came a couple of duns, then Jim's gray,
Pete's sorrel, Lou's black, and way in the back,
  Pájaro, buckskin, and bay.
They had three hundred head of cattle and more:
  forty horses—y mucho dinero![5]
This strange entourage moved like a mirage
  due *south* with that prize-winning "sparrow".

---

1) *Porque*: because.
   Dinero: money.
2) *Cayuse*: Mustang horse.
3) Lou Bailey was a local bartender, Peter Gabriel, a deputy sheriff.
4) *¡Incrédulo!*: Incredible!
5) *Y mucho dinero*: and a lot of money.

The tall one inquired, "Would the locals enjoy a horse race?"

Juegos de los Vaqueros (Games of the Cowboys)

The Mexican cowboy (vaquero) had the utmost influence on the cattle industry of the United States. His manner of working, style of dress, terminology, and even his modes of entertainment had a tremendous effect on the daily life of the American cowboy who is, himself, sometimes referred to as a vaquero.

The vaquero lives a rugged life
With saddle, rope, a gun, a knife.
Clumsy bedroll, ornery steers,
Burning eyes and frozen ears,
Outlaw horses, sweat and tears.
How quick the salary disappears!

Dangerous rivers, Indian foes,
Days and weeks in dirty clothes.
Grimy hair and fingernails,
Loneliness on dusty trails.
When his spirit starts to fail,
Whoops it up and lands in jail!

Days of heat and drought and blood,
Blizzards, rains and desert floods.
What does he for pleasure, then,
To fill the weeks of toiling when
There's naught but cattle, horses, men—
No female 'cept a prairie hen?

Well, here, it seems is what they do
Where simple pleasures seem so few:
There are stories, poems, escapades,
Melodies on mouth harps made,
Songs, and tunes on fiddles played,
Dancing in a masquerade—

The woman's part to thus portray
To mark the close of long hard day.
Drawing lots to see who's bound
The lady's part to thus compound:[1]
A yellow kerchief wrapped around
A fellow's arm. On desert ground

They trip and caper, bow and swing.
Cavort and prance, their bodies fling
Forward, backward, up and down,
Promenade around and round.
With music, laughter night resounds
To dancing on the hard packed ground.

Roping and riding tests become
A way to beat the tedium;
Whether ródeo or rodéo,[2]
It started down in Mexico
Ever and ever so long ago,
Its competitions never slow.

"Los Gallos" was a favored game,[3]
Two men two horses then became—
Each with another piggy-back.
Ready! Set! And then, Attack!
Give the other guy a whack!
Knock him from his "horse's" back!

Jokes, and playing cards and dice.
Shall races—horse and foot—suffice?
Another game some may prefer:
It's called "El gallo" (singular).
A real cock with comb and spur
Up to his neck they will inter

With sand or dirt or gravel 'round
Out upon the open ground.
Two mounted men prepare to ride
Each upon his horse astride,
To dash across arena wide
¡Cuidado, lest the two collide![4]

Pistol's bark! Dash, lean, and snatch!
The rooster's head each tries to catch.
The winner tries to celebrate
But smashing his opponent's pate
With the cock (which he may decapitate—
Or his rival's neck may dislocate).

Thus, we find that not so narrow
¡Son los gustos del vaquero![5]

---

1) "At the smallest ranches dances tended to be sad little affairs with a few fiddles and no women." (William H. Forbes, *The Cowboys,* 1973, op.96); but the shortage of females in the West, both for the military and private sector, did not prevent the men from dancing. In James Michner's *Centennial,* he explains the tradition of "the yellow apron" being used by U.S. Army troops to designate those taking the lady's part, and Candy Moulton (The Writer's Guide to Everyday Life in the Wild West) refers to a handkerchief (probably a yellow neckerchief) on the arms of these "lady folk". The same thing was done by the cowboys. Ramon F. Adams *(Western Words* [Norman, OK, 1944], p. 74) states that a neckerchief tied on the arm of a puncher indicated that he was to "dance lady fashion" and his reward is being allowed to "set with the ladies" between dances This kerchief, was known as the "heifer brand" and must have sometimes been white, as Adams refers to it as "the white emblem of womanhood." Perhaps that is the reason white and yellow neckerchiefs are so uncommon on present day cowboys who sometimes claim they (yellow at least) are bad luck. Men wearing the heifer brand could "take it and pay it back with interest" by dancing "pretty rough" with their male cowboy partners.
2) The word "rodeo" comes from the verb *rodear,* "to go around". In the 1550s it referred to the rounding up of cattle. Later the term came to be associated with the friendly (or perhaps not so friendly) competitions between cowboys on a particular ranch or with neighboring outfits. Skills were matching in roping, riding, and throwing stock. In the United States, the word now refers almost exclusively to the sport rather than the roundup.
3) *Los Gallos*: The Roosters.
4) *¡Cuidado!:* Take care! Be careful! Look out!
5) *Son los gustos del vaquero*: are the pleasures of the cowboy.

Cowboy Preacher

When one young preacher arrived in Charleston, the local rowdies decided to have a good time at the newcomer's expense.

The gunmen were a-gunnin' for the preacher;
Six holes in tall silk hat from shots of lead.
He went in and bought a new 'un—
Low crowned, then said unto 'em,
"Now, boys, there's nothing underneath—
except my head!"

The "new guy" was Amherst graduate A.J. Benedict. His good humored response to the silk hat prank left his tormentors so impressed, they attended his church service that very evening and filled the new hat with money. Benedict became affectionately known as the "Cowboy Preacher."

From a photograph in White family collection, courtesy of Robert Mason, author of *The Burning*.

Annie White

Where the Verde River Flows

This incident occurred near Fort McDowell in July 1880 as related by one of the soldiers who came to the aid of the children involved.

I can hear the children screaming,
The reason I do not know.
The air feels hot and pungent,
In the sky a reddish glow.

Then I see the cloud off toward the north,
Moving upward, dark and slow,
In the shadow of Red Mountain
Where the Verde River flows.

I spur my horse toward the place
Where twisting spirals rise:
Smoke—slowly shifting, drifting
In the copper colored skies,

From the south across the desert.
I draw my kerchief cross my nose,
Mount a rise to view the country
Where the Verde River flows.

I see thirteen mounted soldiers[1]
Riding south back toward the fort;
I see seven frantic children.
And I wonder just what sort

Of thing has just transpired,
And I aim on finding out—
Head down the ridge toward the kids,
As I give a friendly shout.[2]

When I draw near I recognize
The kids—I know their folks:
The children are Patrick and Annie White's,
And they're pointing toward the smoke

That's rising from the desert
About half a mile away;
Household goods are scattered 'round
It's enough to sure convey

The truth of the thing that's happened:
The family's house has been burned down;
The kids been carted there and dumped
On the harsh bare desert ground!

After twenty-one years in the army
Patrick White had now retired
And got him a place close to the fort
Up the Verde a few short miles.

For seven years the Whites had worked
At digging their own canal
To water the crops they'd planted
For pursuits agricultural.

They'd made their living by hauling food
For the soldiers at Fort McDowell.
Milk and eggs and vegetables
And sometimes beef or fowl.

They'd proved up their hundred and sixty,
Six-forty more by the Desert Land Act,[3]
So by the year eighteen-eighty,
They'd quite a substantial tract.

To build a house and keep a few cows,
Annie went to the top position:
The fort's commander, Corliss, she asked
If they might secure permission.

The Captain knew the Whites quite well,
But declared with great conviction
That their spread was off the army base
So he had no jurisdiction.

Why, therefore, this sad situation?
Well, Patrick had been let go
By Corliss's successor,
Just why I still don't know;

But the army said they'd buy no more
Of the produce the White's had grown.
Now, this was pretty hard to take,
For it left them on their own.

Then the new commander of the fort,
Captain Chaffee, said he could prove
That their house was on the army's land![4]
Gave them thirty days to move.

But it hadn't even been two weeks
And their house had been burnt down
And the kids left in the desert
With no adult around—

'Cept me—and I didn't know too much,
(Just a good thing that I'd seen them!)
White and Chaffee, well it sure was true—
There'd been bad blood between them!

Kids said their mama'd gone that day
To Prescott to argue their rights
To the Territorial Governor,
And their daddy was gone for the night—

Camped up where the crew was working
On the canal whence the Verde flows,
There the cottonwood and mesquite are thick
And the palo verde grows.

Annie's sister's family's house was next,
The Carrolls—'twas burned as well;[5]
Both families rendered penniless
By army personnel.

The soldiers and the Apaches
Helped themselves to the stock that strayed.
And Annie? Well, she got nowhere
Though she launched a brave crusade![6]

As you know, the fort was later declared
An Indian reservation,
And healthy sums were offered those
Who lived on the Indian nation;

But the Whites and the Carrolls got nothing,
For the surveys indicated
Their land was outside the boundaries
Of the acreage designated!

What brought about this tragedy?
How did justice go awry?
Who was at fault? Where was the truth?
We may never know who—or why;

But a dream was born and buried,
And the book draws to a close,
Neath the cottonwood and mesquite trees,
Where the Verde River flows.[7]

---

1) Lt. Henry Kendall led the detail of twelve soldiers.
2) Soldiers other than those involved in the burning came to the aid of the stranded children.
3) The Desert Land Act was passed by Congress in 1877, making it possible to acquire an additional six-hundred forty acres, at $1.25 per acre, provided the purchaser would render the land arable within three years.
4) Adna Romanza Chaffee served as commander at Fort McDowell from 1878 to 1882.
5) James Carroll was Annie's sister's husband. He had come from California to assist Patrick in digging what became known as "the White Ditch". The Carroll home was burned in the same manner as the White's and just a month later. Robert Mason in *Verde Valley Lore*, quotes Annie as saying, "Patrick was . . . never again in his right mind." Pat died in 1885.
6) Annie took her family's case all the way to Washington D.C., where she became known as "The Woman With the Black Bag", but no action was ever taken by the government.
7) In his later book, *The Burning* (Phoenix Publishing Group, 2000, p.240), Mason describes a ceremony at the old White Ranch site on October 18, 1905 at which, with bugler and unfurled American flag, a document was read which included the following: "The United States army, in recognition of their error in burning the houses of Mr. and Mrs. Patrick White and Mr. and Mrs. James Carroll in August of 1880, do hereby acknowledge the damage that was done to the White and Carroll properties and present a check in the amount of $45,000 to Mrs. Anna White and a check in the amount of $5,000 to Mr. And Mrs. James Carroll." Interestingly, it was Chaffee (now a General)—who, thirty years previously, had given the order to burn the houses—that signed the reparation document.

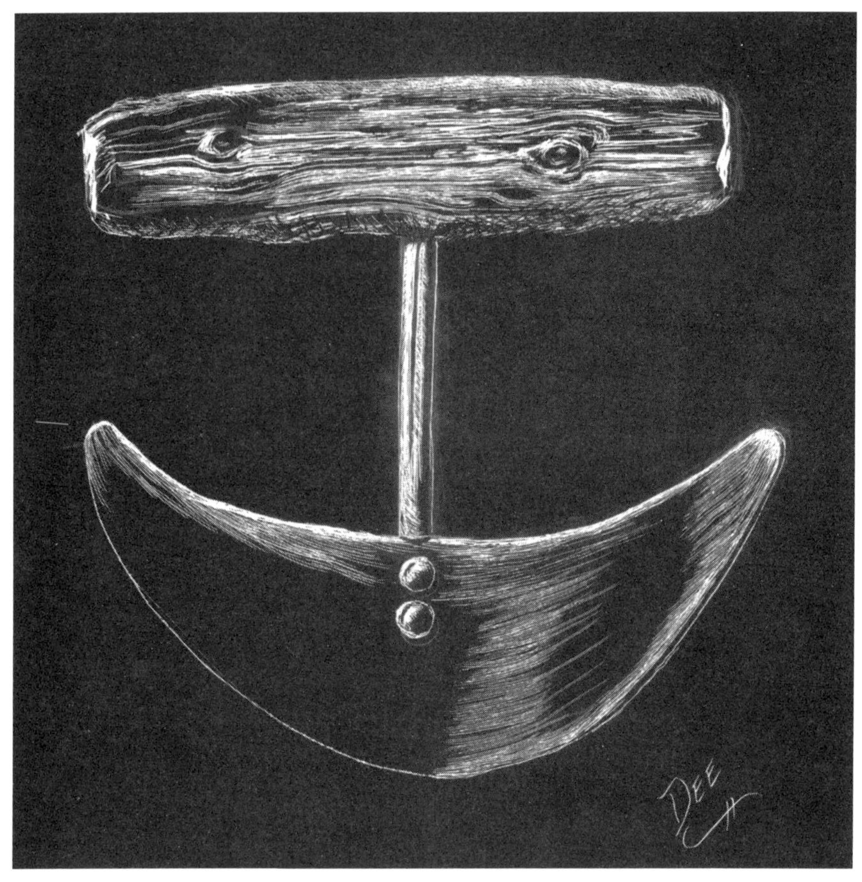

Hash knife used by camp cooks

Them Hash Knife Cowboys

The Aztec Land and Cattle Company came to northern Arizona from Texas in 1885. It was commonly called "The Hash Knife Outfit," for its brand was in the shape of a camp cook's hash knife food chopper. People are resistant to change, but the Aztec boys made a difference. Some Arizona cattlemen stayed with their Spanish (California) traditions; others switched over to Texas methods.

Well, you knew that they came out of Texas—
There's no tellin' where before that,
'Cause most of 'em went by a nickname;
There was dozens of Dicks, Johns, and Pats.

There was Smiths, Joneses, Johnsons aplenty,
I reckon's how that was because
Their other names best be forgotten:
people called them the "Texas Outlaws."

Windy Bob, Loco Tom, Ace of Diamonds,
Poker Bill, the Long and Short Joes;
But nobody asked any questions—
For it wasn't real wise, heaven knows!

Yes, the Aztec came in out of Texas;
Their cowboys was rowdy and bad—
Drivin' cattle that ate less and drank less
Than any cows we'd ever had!

Yet they seemed to produce lots of offspring
And stood up real good to the miles;
And them punchers was durn sure good cowpokes.
We soon was admirin' their style.

They brought us the rim-fired up saddle —
First double rigs we'd ever seen.
We'd always used pure California—
Center fire, single cinch—nice and clean.[1]

They looked at our long tapaderos
That flip-flapped and flopped as we rode;
Called us "chaps, taps and latigo straps'"
And it wasn't too long till we'd stowed

Our seventy foot long reatas[2]
Away with the rest of our gear.
We just gave up takin' our dallies,
All tied hard and fast in a year.[3]

With a 35 foot greasy grass rope.[4]
Why, it looked like a whole different place!
We all bought ourselves Texas saddles,
Accepting the change with good grace.

Yep, we really resented the Hash Knife—
Just a bunch of gun-totin' toughs!
But they changed the way we raised cattle;
They knowed cowboyin' rightly enough!

---

1) Center fire (California rig): Saddle with a single cinch ring placed directly below the saddle-tree.
2) Reata: Braided rawhide rope.
Takin' dallies (dally welta): From Spanish *dar la vuelta*, "to take a turn." Cowboys using this method of securing the lasso by looping it around the saddle horn after the throw had been made.
3) *"Hard and fast"*: Method in which the rope end opposite the loop was tied to the saddle horn.
4) Grass rope: Line made originally of bear grass, later hemp or sisal. Many sources. Jim Bob Tinsley's *Hash Knife Brand* (Gainesille, FL, 1993), *A Dictionary of the Old West* by Peter Watts (New York, 1987), and David Dary, *Cowboy Culture* (New York, 1982).

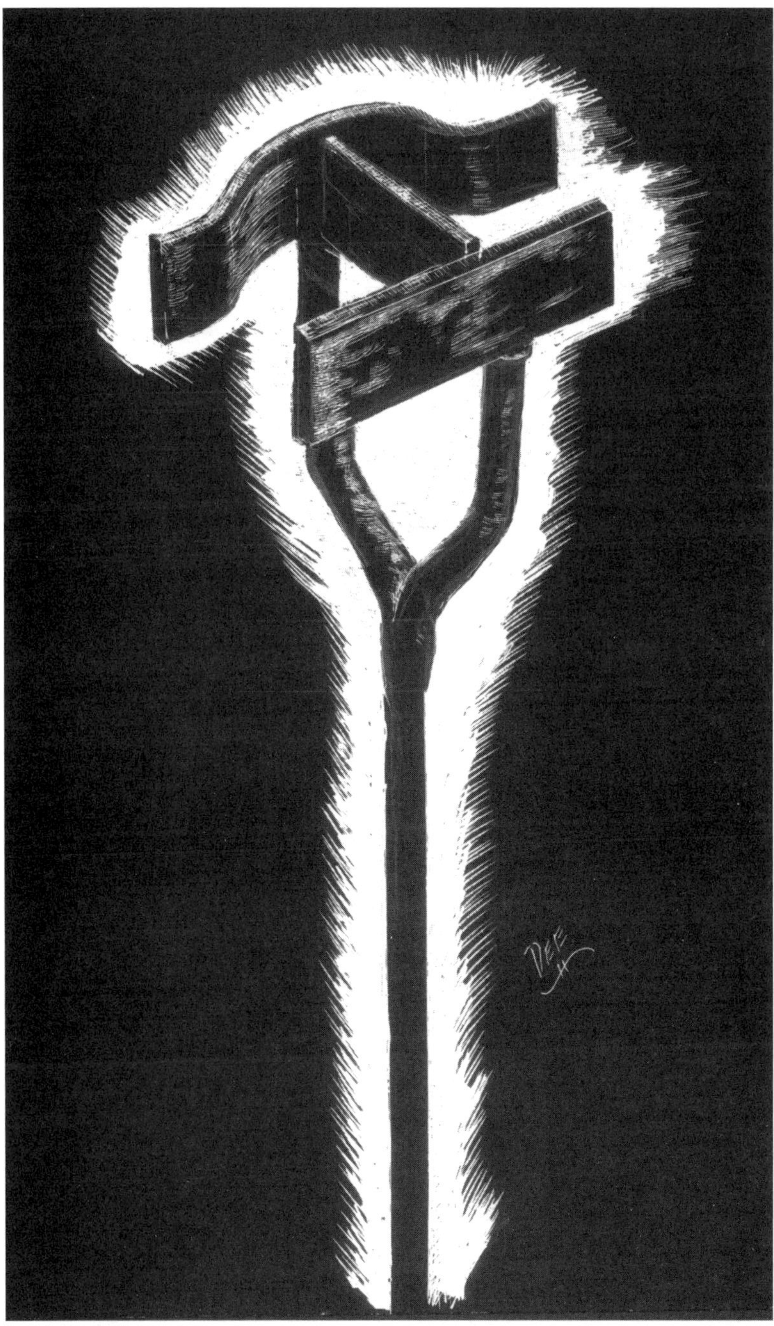

From a photograph by Jim Bob Tinsley, author of *Hash Knife Brand.*

Hash Knife branding iron

Bob Leatherwood's Wager

Bob Leatherwood was elected to the village council of Tucson in 1874. He became mayor in 1880 and remained in public office until 1925, when he lost his bid for sheriff.

Bob was riled up just a smidgen
Cause Jake was arguin' 'bout religion.

Bob says, "There's twenty bucks right there
Says you cain't say the whole Lord's Prayer."

Now big Jake's face lit with a grin
And right away he started in:

"Now I lay me down to sleep,
I pray the Lord my soul to keep. . . ."

"Whoa!" cried Bob, somewhat chagrined,
"That's enough! Dad-gum! You win!"

Tio Pepe (Uncle Joe)

The Atlantic and Pacific railroad was completed as far as Holbrook, Arizona in 1881. A long delay getting across Canyon Diablo prolonged its completion to the western border of the Territory. Land along the railroad right- of-way was sold cheaply to entice settlers to come West. This land was mapped into checker board squares designated odds and evens. Over a million acres of A. and P. land was sold to the big Aztec Land and Cattle Company, which started bringing its herds from Texas into Arizona in 1885. The company was better known as the Hash Knife for its distinctive brand. Even traditional enemies, like small ranchers and sheep men, might find themselves allied against this stronger threat. The incident is fiction, the situation and protagonist, factual.

There's two things I hate, and I reckon its fate
That I've fought with 'em both over land.
One of 'em's sheep (there the conflict runs deep),
And the other's that dang Hash Knife brand.

Them tough Texas boys get most of their joys
From shootin' and rustlin' up stock
That don't wear the Hash; they're rowdy and brash—
We're just lambs in the claws of a hawk.

Lambs? Ha! Therein, I see, that analogy
Recalls them *range maggots* again!
They're the scourge of the plains;
they can wreck the best range.
Its a close-croppin' mealy-mouthed sin!

Well, them Aztec cowpokes had been stirrin' up folks
All across their *million plus* miles—[1]
All that A and P land
that they claimed for their brand,
though our land grants was prev'ously filed.

Why, they took the whole range,
    and it seemed mighty strange
To be left without even the leavin's;
For their sections was odd, but they's ridin' rough shod
    and prohibitin' us from our evens!

But us little guys had begun to get wise—
    bein' strangled to death of our breathin'—
Most good Mormon folks who were sick of the hoax
    and some Baptists and Catholics and heathen.

So the troubles ran deep for both cattle and sheep-
    men who stood in the Aztecers way,
For the Hash Knife was mean—
    that was plain to be seen
        down 'round Canyon Diablo that May.

Well, that caused me one day to be ridin' this way
    where a sheep herder's small flock was staked out,
And across the hills ringin', I heard someone singin'
    though the words, I just couldn't quite make out.

He sure wasn't singin' United States,
    but it wasn't quite Mexican either.
This little old guy with the laughing black eyes,
    just motioned me in for a breather.

Wooly Grower and me, we sat under a tree.
    (I was hard up for allies, of course!)
I could scarcely abide one who smelled of sheep hide,
    but I reckon I smelled like a horse.

He said he was Basque, and he offered his flask,
    which seemed pretty darn decent, you see;
But the comp'ny he'd keep was them dang woolly sheep,
    and that's down right disgustin' to me!

I hated the critter; it made me plumb bitter
    (its part of a cattleman's vows),
But he knew 'em all, and they'd come to his call—
    (and that's more'n I can say for most cows!)

But sheep are dumber than rocks in a dynamite box—
    and I told him so straight to his face.
His dancin' dark eyes opened wide with surprise;
    He sez, "No, Señor, no es la case"—

Or somethin' like that; then he took off his hat,
    and he said, "Tio Pepe my name is."[2]
Why, I laughed till I cried at that wool pusher's lies;
    at tall tales he'd ought to be famous!

He knowed stories and songs,
    and I might have been wrong,
But his truths seemed as sound as the gospel.
    He could cheer up a snake, so for my own sake,
        I tracked him down's often as poss'ble.

So I made my best friend, one I'd keep to the end—
    "Tio Pepe," whose right name was Pablo—
A dang muttoneer—honest, gentle, sincere,
    (but don't tell the boys at Diablo!)

---

1) The speaker is exaggerating slightly.
2) Tio Pepe Martinéz was an actual Basque sheepherder, the great uncle of my cousin Andrew Martin, to whom I dedicate this poem. (Note the accent on the *final* syllable of Pepe's last name. Many of the Martinéz family changed their name to Martin because they did not wish to called *Martínez*).

Destination Phoenix

Corp. William Bladen Jett was discharged from the army at Fort Huachuca in April, 1886. After working awhile in southern Arizona, he decided to go investigate Phoenix. As the railroad spur between Phoenix and Maricopa was not completed until July, 1887, it was necessary for Phoenix-bound passengers to find their own transportation the rest of the thirty five miles from Maricopa. Use of the German accent is in no way intended as disrespect of the German people.

We were stuck in Maricopa,
Having come in on the train,
Me and and this big German guy,
Whose face looked struck with pain

When he learned the town of Phoenix
Was thirty-five miles due north;
No train nor bus for either of us,
So we'd just as well set forth.

We were walkin' down the dusty road,
When much to our surprise,
A lumber wagon lumbered up,
A sight for sun burned eyes!

The teamster told us, for a fee,
To Phoenix he would take us,
The rate was high, but Fritz and I
Could not afford a fracas.

One dollar fifty cents we paid!
Now, for that kind of money
We should have had a meal or two
But that was down right funny!

Three times we had to shovel sand
To loose the wagon wheels,
And if you've never done such work,
I can tell you how it feels!

We bumped and rattled till night came;
Then, there beside the road,
We stretched ourselves out on the ground
Like three big horny toads.

The driver and me, when morning broke,
Climbed back in the wagon seat.
"Geddap!" he hollered to the mules,
(I sure would've liked to eat!)

We left the German sound asleep,
But he woke up with a jolt
When we had driven fifty yards.
You'd ought to've seen him bolt!

"Hey! Whoa, der, Herr mule drivuh!
Stop! Whoa dem dumkoff mules!
How come you do not wake up Fritz?
You take me for a fool?"

Draggin' his blankets the feller ran,
I reckon he cussed in German,
"I pay you Phoenix for to go!"
He sounded right determined.

He jumped up on the wagon;
Driver offered nary booster,
Sez, "Yeah. You didn't pay me, though,
To be no dad-burned rooster!"

Jett, William Bladen. *"The Reluctant Corporal," The Autobiography of William Bladen Jett,* pt. 2, ed. Henry Pl. Walker. *The Journal of Arizona History,* XII, 2 (Summer 1971), pp. 123.

Leaving Phoenix

After trying his hand at ranching and mule skinning, William Bladen Jett went to Phoenix. By 1888, when Jett felt he had been called to preach and decided to return to Virginia to pursue his theological studies, the spur railroad to Maricopa was newly completed. From there, a passenger could travel to Tucson, catch the Southern Pacific, and proceed east.

I was sleeping on the depot floor
in Phoenix, Arizona,
Waiting for the midnight train
To come and take me over
The Mississippi River,
back home to old Virginny;
There beside me lay a guy,
plumb scatterbrained and skinny.

He said he was from Texas,
bound to quit this territory.
Goin' back to where he come from;
spoke in terms derogatory
Of this here place called Phoenix.
I asked him why he's leaving
He sez, "It's too dang muddy here!"
I thought my ears deceiving!

"Why, it never even rains here!
So what's your line of thinking?"
(I thought this crazy Texan
Must surely have been drinking!)
"But it dang sure will rain someday!"
Sez he, "You kain't ignore it!
This place will sure be muddy then!
And I ain't stayin' for it!"

William Bladen Jett, p. 140.

The Other Mother

Dedicated to the mother of Jeff (Billy) Wilson, the "unknown cowboy," who was hanged by a mob on top of the Mogollon Rim, together with Jamie Stott and Jim Scott in August, 1888, as described in the poem "The Hangin' Tree" in the previous section.*

And what of the other cowboy?
 The one that they called "unknown"?
He had to have come from somewhere,
 To have been some mother's own.
He had to have been a child once,
Though tall and calloused grown.

Did she die as he came into being?
 Was the baby's first gasp of breath
The mother's last? Did she whisper,
 As she lay in the arms of death,
"See that my child is christened,
 For my father—name him Jeff."

Or did she die when he was a child?
 Did he flee to the woods half grown,
So no one could see a "big boy" cry,
 And to mourn his loss alone?
Or did he break his mother's heart
 As young people often do
By heading for Arizona
 To become a buckaroo?

Then doubtless she never heard the truth,
  And likely she never knew
What became of him she loved so well;
  Of the stately pine which grew
On the rim of a far off canyon,
  As a wild wind, wailing, blew,
Stirring the limp and lifeless forms
  Of three young buckaroo.

Did she pray each day for her missing son?
  Did she sing by the lamp light's glow
"*O, Where is My Wandering Boy Tonight*"?
  Did she whisper it soft and slow,
And wonder why the wind sang back
  "*It is best that you do not know.*"

---

* The "unknown cowboy": Phrase used by Leland J.Hanchett, Jr. in *Crooked Trail to Holbrook.*

Belle of the Bar

'Twas a cold dark night in Prescott,
    January 'ninety-eight,
The saloon quite populated
    For a snowy night so late,
The bar and tables crowded,
Loud music, laughter, smoke.
The smell of men and liquor
    Was enough to make one choke.

The "sweet singer" sure was "holding sway
    On the stage of the Cabinet Saloon."[1]
The piano was loud and so was the crowd
    As she rendered them forth a tune.
Yes, the place was a din. A veiled woman walked in.
    Frank Williams, the barkeep, was stunned,
For she boosted her bundle up onto the bar
    And left in a fast limping run.

Well, it didn't take long to disrupt the song;
    Abruptly, the very air changed.
Frank pulled back the cover, there to discover
    A baby! How shocking and strange!
A brief heavy hush. Then all the men rushed
    And pressed toward that end of the bar,
The miners, the ranchers, the railroaders came—
    All those who most usually are

The drinkers and gamblers on tough Whiskey Row.
    In such rowdy and rough atmosphere
Of vice-filled saloons, full of smoke and spittoons,
    Could an innocent angel appear?
All "business was brought to a standstill" it's said,[2]
    An electric shock ran through the bar.
So strong were the vibes that it's hard to describe
    Excitement so high and bizarre!

The boys in the back room came hurrying out
Just as Frank was conscripted to read
The note that he'd found
in the cloth wrapped around
The baby; and so proceeds:
"'*This little baby belongs to John Bell,*
Give her to him, or call in the law.
The woman who cared for her's down awful sick;
She can't do no more.' Boys, that's all!"

Now, John Bell had been known
To frequent that place,
But he hadn't been seen for awhile;
And nobody offered to go look him up;
Each face was just lit by a smile.
Why, you never saw such a gaggle of guys
Act so foolish to make a child laugh!
They gobbled and gooed and played peek-a-boo.
(Would have made a great photograph!)

For just like the miners of rough *Roaring Camp,*[3]
The tough lot was transformed by the sight
Of a sweet little child—who had them beguiled:
The Belle of the Bar that cold night!
Yes, the wee tot was certainly touching the heart
Of every old sinner man jack.
She cooed and she smiled;
Their hard hearts beguiled
And they all "cooed like fools" right back.[4]

Then somebody hollered, "Let's gamble for her!
Each toss of the dice is ten bucks!"
And so all agreed; it was something indeed—
More than forty men trying their luck.[5]
Conversation was thin as the money rolled in.
Intent were the eyes of each man
Which they were unable to take from the table
As the dice rattled out of the can.

It took quite awhile; a frown followed a smile,
As a high count was beat. Man alive!
Frank pronounced we were done
And announced Bob had won.
"Full house! Three sixes, two fives."
But as the old bachelor stepped up for his prize,
A man entered, all covered with snow.
Robert Groom was denied,
For Judge Hicks had arrived,[6]
And announced, "Boys, I'll have the last throw!"

They gave him the can, and every last man
Heard the rattle and roll of the dice.
Five sixes! He'd won! The old son-of-a-gun!
(Some claimed that the dice rolled "too nice").[7]

They gave him the baby as well as the cash:
About four hundred dollars, I'm told!
He promised each cent on her would be spent—
The bills and the silver and gold.

Bob was unreconciled, but the judge got the child,
And took her straight home to his wife.
And many inquired as to what there transpired.
(Most explaining he'd done in his life!)

Now some people say that they named the girl *Chance*,
Because of the way he'd acquired her,
But in fact, it was *Violet* Hicks chose for her name,
And he loved her as if he had sired her.[8]

But most of us still call her *Sweet Baby Bell*,
She is known thus at home and afar,
For those who were there on that cold winter's night
Proclaimed her the *Belle of the Bar!*[9]

---

1) From *The Journal Miner*, January 26, 1898. Sources which place the event at the *Palace* Saloon are incorrect. (Leo Banks, "*The Saga of an Abandoned Baby*," *Rattlesnake Blues*, pp. 90).

2) The *Journal Miner*, ibid.

3) A reference to Bret Harte's well known story, "The Luck of Roaring Camp" which had appeared in *The Overland Monthly* in 1868.

4) Banks, "*The Saga of an Abandoned Baby*," *p.* 86.

5) "Not less than forty men": *The Evening Courier* (January 1898), quoted by Banks, pp.86.
6) Robert Groom (1824-1899) had mining claims in the pine-covered area south of Prescott, now called Groom Creek. He was also the surveyor who laid out the plan for the town of Prescott. Several descendants of Judge Charles P. Hicks (1858-1929) have gone into dentistry in the Prescott area.
7) "Rolled too nice": an inference to loaded dice.
8) Edmund Wells in *Argonaut Tales,* copyright 1927, states that the child was named *Chance of Cobweb Hall* because she was won, by a roll of the dice, in the *Cobweb Hall Saloon* (one of forty bars on Whiskey Row), and adopted by Judge Charles Hall (rather than Charles *Hicks*). Wells claimed to have been present the night of the incident, yet, upon investigation, it seems that his memory failed him with respect to the names of the saloon, the judge, and the child. (Banks, *Rattlesnake Blues*, p. 84).
9) Violet Hicks moved to California where she married Arthur Binner, whom she later divorced. They had four children. Violet died in Redwood City, October 12, 1970 at the age of seventy two.

Slim Woman: Asthon Sosi

Louisa Wade married John Wetherill in 1896. When he decided to become an Indian trader, she went with him to New Mexico and Arizona. She learned to speak Navajo fluently and was highly respected among the Navajo people. She died in 1945, a year after her husband. Parts of this poem take place in Colorado, New Mexico and Utah, rather than Arizona, but in the Four Corners area, the land is all one—Navajo.[1]

I. Acquisition of a Name

Reared in southwest Colorado,
Miss Wade wed a Quaker named John.
They slaved at their farm,
 but drought did them harm,
And at last they were forced to move on.

John Wetherill, like his brother Ben,[2]
Had lived 'mongst the Navajos.
He told her of silver and turquoise skills
And the fine woolen rugs that they wove.

With their children and Louisa's young brother,
They moved south to begin a new life
In the colorful land of the Navajo clans,
Indian trader with family and wife.

First they lived way up north of Gallup,
Where they started their Navajo trade.
When John was away for days upon days,
Louisa and little ones stayed.

At first she feared about being alone
In this desolate, arid wasteland;
No husband or mother, just her young brother
And kids, two and four, there at hand.

She learned to speak the basic words:
Such as numbers, and *goat skin,* and *rug,*
Silver and *swap, coffee, sugar,* and *pop*—[3]
Or just spoke with a nod or a shrug.

But once when John was away from the post
Her young brother fell gravely ill,
But inadequate to communicate
With her limited language skills,

She tried asking the Indians who came and went
To locate her parents or John.
Worn, spent and crying, as her brother lay dying,
She seemed lacking the strength to fight on.

A trader who happened to pass that way
Got the Indians to understand.
Soon her parents arrived, and the brother survived;
But that was enough! She now planned

To gain enough skill in the language
To speak to the people around her,
To stop fearing dangers and be, to these strangers,
A friend and a neighbor; they found her

Wise, warm, willing and eagerly bright,
Right quickly she comprehended.
The language she learned and she rapidly earned
The respect of the folk she'd befriended.

Their conversations she soon understood;
She cherished their songs and their stories.
She spoke Navajo, that strange language so
Full of nuance and allegory.[4]

Asthon Sosi, the Navajos called her,
This trader's wife, slender and young;
For she had achieved what few white men conceived:
Command of the Navajo tongue!

She listened to *the People,*[5]
She worshipped their land from her door.
She treasured their kindness, amazed at the blindness
That had kept her from seeing before

Their beauty and their dignity,
Their humor and fine way of life.
She loved their lore and their legends and swore
To assist them in all of their strife;

For the Navajos were a nation
Who walked in a sort of twilight,
Confused and forlorn, for its people were torn
Between cultures—the red and the white.

II. Moonlight Waters

Then the land to the west—Arizona—
Beckoned its finger to John.
There the whites were mistrusted;
Indians felt they all lusted

After land for their ranches and farms.
For too well *the Dineh* remembered
Gaunt specters in bas-relief,
When the People were crying, as hundreds fell dying
From exposure and hunger and grief.[6]

So they shook their heads at the trader,
Saying, "No, you White Eyes, turn back!"
But in his gentle way, the Quaker would say
"Look, Hosteen, I come as a friend."[7]

He invited them all to have dinner;
He cooked them a good rabbit stew,
Coffee, sugar and bread, the whole outfit fed;
Told them *these* he'd provide for *them* too.

So the Indians accepted this white man,
And he started a trading post there
At Kayenta (which means *moonlight waters)*
Which his *Slim Woman* came to share.

That name, *Asthon Sosi,* persisted;
Through domain of the Navajo—
It spread o'er the sand that makes up the land,
For the natives respected her so.

Also called *Sister,* or *Mother*
By this people she'd now come to know;
"*Granddaughter,*" said Chief Hoskinini;
"It's sure that her soul's Navajo."

These were her friends and companions,
And they came to her for advice.
She settled disputes with wisdom astute;
She seemed such a part of their life.

III. Rediscovering the Rainbow:

John loved nature's peculiar stone sculptures,
And she'd heard of a unique formation
Not far from the valley of monuments,
Far north on the reservation.

She told him the Navajos spoke of a bridge
Once sacred but, sadly, now lost,
Since the People were shedding their native beliefs.
(O, who could have counted the cost!)

So Louisa told John the story,
Of a time once, long long ago,
When a miracle formed a natural bridge
In the shape of a great granite bow.

John was intrigued by the story;
He, at last, an old Navajo found
Who recalled that once in the days of his youth,
He had stood on the then sacred ground

Below the great red stone rainbow
Which he and his cousin had seen
As they were out chasing wild horses —
Now, completely forgotten, it seemed,

Was the location of the formation;
But John hired himself a guide,
And they rode on up into Utah
Toward the place the old man had described.

At last they located the rainbow
Which the People had somehow misplaced,
And restored to them their priceless gem,
Their sacred rainbow place.

Years later a U.S. President[8]
Stood beside the great arch of stone,
And John was honored for finding the bridge,
But Louisa, said, No! Not alone

Had he found the long lost Rainbow Bridge,
And insisted the government plaque
List not only John's name, but that of the guide
Who had helped to bring the shrine back

To the disturbed and distracted Navajos;
And she also insisted that there
The Chant of the Lost must be written,
The young chieftain's death song prayer.[9]

---

1) Anderson, Dorothy Daniels. *Arizona Legends and Lore: Tales of Southwestern Pioneers* (Phoenix,1995), pp. 114-128.
2) Benjamin Alfred Wetherill is credited as the first white man to see the "Cliff Palace" of Mesa Verde.
3) Soft drink, *soda water,* was developed in the 1890s. It acquired the name "pop" because of the sound made when original caps were removed. It was never referred to as "soda" in the area of Arizona where the author grew up. This term was used only by tourists.
4) John never acquired the proficiency of Louisa for the Navajo tongue, but the Navajos accepted and respected him for his honesty and kindness.
5) The Navajos call themselves *Dineh,* "the people".
6) Navajos had been relocated into northern New Mexico. The "long walk" to Bosque Redondo (Round Forest) was begun in January, 1863 and continued for a year. The cold of winter and the heat of summer took their toll. The Indians suffered greatly.
7) *Hosteen* (Navajo): Mister.
8) President Theodore Roosevelt declared Rainbow Bridge a national monument in 1910.
9) See "*Legend of the Rainbow*" in the "Legends and Lore" section, which follows.

From photographs in the Wetherill family collection, courtesy of Dorothy Daniels Anderson, author of *Arizona Legends and Lore*.

Louisa Wade Wetherill with Sam Chief family

The Question of the Cow

The Navajos respected "Asthon Sosi" so highly, she was often called upon to settle disputes among them.

"You killed my cow!" said the Navajo,
As he glared at the young Paiute.

"It was a real *old* cow," replied the Paiute,
"Not worth the powder to shoot!"

"A good *young* cow!" insisted the first,
The best one that I ever had!"

"She wasn't worth nothing! So skinny and old!
What's it matter?" the Paiute said.

"You know she was young!" the Navajo cried.
"You butchered her there in the canyon!"

(For this he had seen with his two good eyes:
The Paiute with a companion).

"I pay him a dollar." The Paiute smiled.
"Two dollars if that's what it takes!

"For though she was old and not worth a cent,
She did make us pretty good steaks!"

"You killed my best cow! You owe me a horse
Or another good cow! You must pay!"

"That scrawny old cow was not worth a horse!
And I'm not giving *good* cows away!"

So they argued there in Slim Woman's house:
Fifteen Indians from each of the tribes,
Three hours or more the wrangling went on
Each eager, indeed, to describe

The appearance and disappearance
  Of the disputed departed cow.
The matter had to be settled, for sure;
  The question, of course, was *how*?

They turned to the slender white lady,
  "Asthon Sosi, we'll be here all night.
Tell us what we must do about this dead cow.
  Otherwise, we'll just have to fight!"

Louisa had listened carefully
  To the statements presented by each;
She weighed the issues on both of the sides,
  And this was her ultimate speech:

"Remember, Hosteen, when my colt was lost,
  And later you found some horse bones?
You said it probably *was* my colt,
  And the way that this was known

"Was the fact that the bones were yellow—
  You said from a *young* horse, right?
You explained that in an older colt,
  The bones would be thin and white."

She looked at opposing factions,
  Both were nodding agreement to this.
If the bones were white, the cow was old:
  Result of metastasis.

"Each side must now choose one person," she said,
  "Who will do as he is told:
Each will bring back a rib from the cow that's dead,
  Then we'll know: was she *young* or *old*?"

Then quickly the Paiute defendant spoke up
In a voice of considerable force:
"We don't need to ride for the bones," he said.
"I'll go home and get him a horse!"

Anderson, pp.125-126.

From a photograph by Barry Goldwater, Goldwater Collection, Arizona Historical Foundation.

Hosteen

IV. Legends, Lore, Myths & More: From Who Knows When?

"Much lore we leave you worth the knowing; much much has lain outside our ken."

— Thomas Hardy

"A curious legend still haunts me, still haunts and obsesses my brain."

— Heinrich Heine

Poems are arranged with legends and lore first, then lies and practical jokes, and finally, unlikely stories told as fact.

The Legend of the Rainbow

Once, oh now, so very long ago,
There walked upon the earth a young chieftain;
There walked a young man pleasing to the gods.
And Young Man loved the earth, his Mother Earth,
and treated her with care and deep respect.

One day a gentle rain began to fall.
Young Man was glad, because his Mother Earth
Was dry and very thirsty, and the rain,
Falling on the parched and barren ground,
sweetened the air about, with cleansing breath,

But the rain did not stop; it continued to fall,
And Earth was not able to swallow it up.
It fell on the desert and on the wild grass.
On the river and on the small streams,
The water gathered quickly and they rose.

The waters rose, and Young Man said, "It rains.
I must run until I find a higher place,
For water will soon cover all the plain."
The waters did just as the chieftain said:
the waters rose and covered the flat prairie,

The desert, and the pastures, and the fields.
Higher and higher the great waters rose;
Faster the sure-footed Young Man ran
Till he reached a little rise, and there he stood,
waiting till the fierce storm should subside.

But rain continued; still the waters rose,
Washing over the tops of his moccasins.
Young man felt fear no man should ever feel.
And looking about him thought,
"Where shall I run?"

Across the valley stood a sheer steep cliff,
Above the cliff a high and stony plain.
If he could reach that place he would be safe;
But the waters were too swift for him to swim,
    and the cliff was far too high for him to climb.

Facing the North, Young Man began to chant.
He cried out to the Spirits of North,
"Great North Wind! Send a bridge that I may climb
High above the waters and be saved!"
Yet harsher blew the breath of old North Wind.

Strong blew the wind, the mighty, cold North Wind.
The waters rose, this time to Young Man's knees.
Chanting, he turned himself toward the East.
"Oh, Spirit of the East Wind, send a bridge!"
    and great winds blew from out the clouded East.

Soon waters swirled about brave Young Man's waist.
To Spirits of the South and West he prayed,
"A rainbow! Send a rainbow I can climb!"
Then winds began to howl from out the West,
And also from the South and North and East.

"A rainbow! Send a rainbow I can climb!"

Winds wailed and screeched, and turbulence arose,
And dark mists hovered over all the Earth.
Now Young Man prayed the Death Chant of the Lost.
The deep and soulful Death Chant of the Lost.

Strange colors whirled amongst the murky mists.
Then swirled the darksome rain clouds into form,
Converting to a bow above his head!
A great transparent rainbow o'er his head!
And, slowly, then the darkness did subside;
    The colored light grew solid and became

A bridge of stone, a bright vermilion orange.
A Rainbow Bridge
    to save him from the flood.
        Great Rainbow Bridge
            to save him from the flood!

Anderson, *Arizona Legends*, pp. 122-123.

Peralta Gold

Don Miguel, on his Mexican rancho,
Lived high on society's ranch, though
He hungered for more to add to his store
A la villa del Señor Peralta
Which was well known in that territory,
Truly splendid in all of its glory!
'Twas famous for miles, though great were the trials
Of running the rancho Peralta.

A beautiful young señorita
('Twas Don Miguel's daughter, Rosita),
Fell in love—(was it chance?)—with a hand at the ranch
Who worked for the great Don Peralta.
Don Miguel upon finding this fact out
Decided his fury to act out,
But the lover took flight, riding into the night,
"Track the dog!" screamed el Señor Peralta.

Two riders pursued the young lover
Who spurred the south wind to seek cover,
Riding north toward the place where the ominous face
Of a great granite mountain loomed starkly.[1]
Several days his pursuers kept tracking
Though chance of success seemed quite lacking.
Then one night by fire light, he stepped out of the night
Where the cliffs and the canyons loomed darkly.

O'er his head his arms were extended,
As if to say, "No harm intended."
And each hand, it's told, held a nugget gold
That gleamed in the flickering fire light.
Said he, "There's a great peak of gold near.
If you spare me, we three can take hold here.
We can stake us a claim; we can gain wealth and fame!"
So they talked through the rest of the long night.

Next morning he showed them the region
Where gold ore and nuggets were legion.
They filled up their packs with rich gold to take back
When they rode out again to the prairie.
For they'd worked on a waterless mountain,
No springs and no thirst quenching fountain.
So they planned out their course, packing onto each horse,
As much gold that the poor beast could carry.

They put gold in an old Indian olla,
Which they buried and planted with cholla
To cover the space, then they smoothed out the place
And reluctantly they departed.
Now, close by their mine, like an arrow,
Was a spire they called Mina Sombrero,[2]
A pinnacle that they thought looked like a hat.
Then they felt their course safely charted,

They rode from the ominous cliffs then,
Thinking how they would someday be rich! When
A rain-swollen stream quickly ended that dream,
Swept away in the thundering flood there!
Only one dragged himself from the torrent,
From that gold-sodden death-trap abhorrent,
The others were gone, and the one who lived on
Found the corpse of the lover in mud there.

He took all the gold he could carry
But he knew he must find sanctuary.
He decided to chance going back to the ranch,
Peralta must honor his story!
The vaquero was right in his theory:
Stumbling, staggering, weary,
He arrived at the villa, gasped, "Agua fria!"
And fell with the gold from his quarry.

He rasped out his tale to Peralta
Who quietly whispered "No faulta."
Though he'd failed in his quest, the vaquero was blessed
By magnanimous Señor Peralta.
Rosita was quietly weeping
As she thought how her lover lay sleeping.
Her father's one mission—to send expeditions
To gain greater wealth for Peralta!

Three missions returned with great treasure
Which Peralta received with great pleasure.
The gold he so prized, that he soon organized
The greatest of all expeditions!
He'd heard of Apache exertions
To end such Hispanic excursions.
No matter what cost, lest the mountain be lost,
He must act, for he saw his position!

He gathered four hundred vaquero,
Plus a thousand beasts, to his ranchero;
They then started forth, this large train, toward the north,
For the peak that looked like a sombrero.
No sooner had this expedition
  set forth by Peralta's ambition,
Than the Indians found out, and forthwith set about
An ambush in a mountain pass narrow.

Fierce eyes scowled down on the companions
As they moved through the harrowing canyons.
A frontal attack! Also one from the back!
And the Mexican train was surrounded![3]
The Apache warriors' shrill crying
Were mingled with screams of the dying,
Peralta's fine train seemed every man slain
E'er the Indians' retreat cry was sounded.[4]

Don Miguel, on his Mexican rancho,
Lived high on society's branch, though
He hungered for more to add to his store
For the villa of Señor Peralta.
But Peralta's glory was ended.
The Apaches their mountain defended.
Thus it had begun—and now it was done,
That's the tale of the gold of Peralta![5]

---

1) Mountains now called the Superstitions, east of Phoenix.
2) La Mina Sombrero (the hat mine)—the "hat" was, perhaps, Weaver's Needle.
3) The assault was launched by the combined warriors of Apache leaders Mangas Colorados (Red Sleeves) and Cochise.
4) Some say two escaped. With night falling,
They, miraculously, by swift crawling,
Hid themselves in the brush in the darkening hush,
As the moans and the groans fell to silence.
The least wounded, then, helped his companion
Slip away along the dim canyon
From the grim, gruesome sight. All through the long night,
Their minds reeled in turmoils of violence.
5) Is there truth to the story? Who knows? In *Arizona Legends and Lore*, Dorothy Daniels Anderson tells the fine tale as if it were fact, stating that Don Miguel Peralta's rancho was located in Sonora, and the events described in the poem took place in the 1840s. There have been, of course, a number of Miguel Peraltas. Marshall Trimble, Arizona's Official Historian, refers to several in various books. One came to Arizona from California, having not done too well there during the gold rush of 1849. He staked a claim in Yavapai County. Another had a mercantile business in Phoenix in the early 1870s. The best known Miguel Peralta, however, was fictitious, the child of the fertile unscrupulous brain of James Addison Reavis, "The Baron of Arizona" who arrived in Tucson in 1882. None of the authentic Reavises appear to have been related to Elisha Reavis, hermit of the Superstition Mountains.

The Mysterious Lady in Blue

The story of the miraculous lady in blue exists in the lore of many Southwestern tribes: Zuni, Pima, Apache, Tejas and others.

To a mission in sixteen eighty-nine
Came a Tejas Chief, straight and proud,
Requesting a bolt of sky blue cloth,
His mother's corpse to enshroud.

The priest there attempted to explain
That *black* was the hue for the dead,
But the Chief insisted on "*blue*, like the sky".
He'd accept nothing else, he said.

A tale from their lore, oft repeated before:
A white lady in long gown of blue
Had come to their village and told them of Christ
Many years before padres came through.

She came there to preach, to baptize and teach;
She miracles sometimes performed.
Why, to this very day, there are Indians who say
She came to their ancestral homes.

She always talked in the language they spoke—
The people to whom she came.
Always described as "the lady in blue",
Though no one discovered her name.

Fray Alonzo de Benevides described
How to him, some natives had come.
He said they became excited when they
Saw a painting there of a nun.

"Our lady in blue wore a robe like this!"
Enthusiastically they had begun;
Then they proceeded to tell him their tale,
Just as the others had done.

Fray Alonzo felt sure that no nuns had arrived
Before the year sixteen thirty-two,
Yet between twenty-nine and sixteen thirty-one
Had appeared the strange lady in blue.

When Father Alonzo journeyed to Spain,
To the church at Agreda he went.
This order, he knew, wore habits of blue,
As they worked and prayed at the convent.

To the Mother Superior he asked to speak.
There, Maria de Jesus presided,
The youngest of all to be so assigned,
And to him this dear lady confided:

Long she had envied the roles of the priests
Being sent to New Spain's southwest,
And, hesitantly, she told of strange dreams
In which her desire, unexpressed,

Was always fulfilled. She spoke of the times
She had dreamt about strange layered towns,
Of telling the story of Christ in his glory
To people with skins reddish-brown.

With accuracy she described their quaint homes—
The pueblos the padre knew well—
Of which no white soul, save himself, should have known.
How was it this young nun could tell

So precisely how the buildings appeared,
The people and the terrain?
How had the woman acquired these facts?
He viewed the whole thing with disdain.

Checking the records, he found that no nun
Had from that stoic place been away
A sufficient time to have gone and returned.
Had she learned it from books in some way?

No theory seemed to provide him the clue
In that secluded and cloistered place.
Reincarnation? Out of body affair?
The church would have frowned in the face

Of such an idea! 'Twas evil! Occult!
Fray Alonzo admonished his friend
To pray that these dreams would cease and desist,
That such longings and yearnings would end.

The good lady prayed that some other dreams
Would these wandering pictures replace;
But as visions like those began to subside,
Weird nightmares appeared in their place.

Father Kino records the last sighting of
The wonderful lady in blue:
A visit to Pimaría again,[1]
But it differed from those hitherto:

An elderly Pima man there recalled
That many years previously
A young white lady in flowing blue robes
Had appeared most mysteriously.

At first she spoke in a gentle soft voice
In the tongue they could understand,
Then, in some strange language, began to shout,
Which frightened the peaceable band!

The warriors shot her with arrows, he said.
There she fell, and believing her dead,
The Pimas all left that unholy place,
Quickly gathered their children and fled.

Could this strange phenomenon be the same
As the dream of Maria Jesus?
Had some strange nun really wandered among
The Indians? Could it be abuse

Of God's holy vows? No nuns in New Spain!
The church in Old Spain had confirmed!
So who was the strange young woman in blue
Whose appearance Indians affirmed?

The Lady Returns

One hundred and sixty years later, there came
To Sonora, American troops,
A journey of filibuster it was.
(Only one survived from this group.)[2]

He said when they tried to blow up the church,
A lady in robes of light blue,
Appeared before the men with the guns
And quietly put out the fuse.

This action repeated a half dozen times,
Then the soldiers were overtaken.
And all were killed by the Mexican men,
Save one—and the venture forsaken.[3]

The lady in blue—could she have been
The same that before was discerned
By Indians, oh, many long years before?
No one has, as yet, ever learned.

---

1) Pimaría Alta: What is now northern Sonora and southern Arizona. In this area diverse groups of Pima peoples resided. It was to these people that Father Eusebio Kino ministered, and where he built twenty-four missions from 1687 to 1711.
2) This filibuster expedition, led by Henry Crabb, descended upon Sonora in 1857, in an effort to take the state. The filibuster was put down by Mexican troops at Caborca.
3) Only the fifteen-year-old sharpshooter, Charlie Evans, was spared. It was he who gave the report of the conclusion of the ill fated expedition and the miraculous intercession at the church. He said the expedition had buried a large amount of gold before attacking the church, and that he himself found it, later offering it to his captors, with whose cause he had come to agree. (Griffith, James S. Introduction to Margaret Proctor Redondo's "*Valley of Iron.*" *The Journal of Arizona History*, XXXIV: 3 [Autumn 1993], pp. 233-237.

The Legend of La Llorona

The tale of La Llorona, the weeping woman, is prevalent all over the Southwest—wherever Mexican people dwell. The location and the details of her story vary, but one thing is consistent: a woman's ghost weeps for the children she has drowned. (Glossary follows poem)[1]

Have you heard the tales of the woman who wails
On the banks of the Rio Grande?
(Or is it the Gila or Santa Cruz
Colorado or Contrabande?)[2]

I've heard the tale told by men who sought gold,
by their campfire's flickering light,
In cantinas dim, and under the rim
in the gray hours before day light.

And as oft' when guards change
by men of the range,
uneasy in high-backed kaks, as[3]
By flickering lamps in the timber camps
where the lumberjacks swing their axes.

It's that mournful wail that makes the trail
so fearful for native or stranger;
For the fact is known that a man alone
rides threatened by mortal danger.

It will soon be shown—he who rides alone
near the banks of a swift flowing stream
May very well drown—in the waters go down
like a child in a hideous dream.

¡Venga, compadre! ¡Adios a su madre!
You're one I shall tell the tale to
Of what haunts the bleak hills
where the Mexican dwells.
¡Cuidado! A weak heart may fail you!

A young woman fair (¡Que bonita mujer!),
A flashing-eyed dark señorita,
Fell 'neath the spell of a rash ne'er-do-well.
¡Muy triste la mujer bonita!

Two children she bore, but the bold matador,
or whoever he was, had absconded;
And she mourned him at night
by the moon's eerie light,
but only the river responded.

And so, thus estranged, her mind was deranged,
And her thoughts with revenge were absorb-ed.
¡Ah, it chills me to speak of something so bleak!
¡So frightful! ¡So awful! ¡So morbid!

For her niños she drowned
As the waters rolled down;
Beneath the brown billows they perished.
Hear her pitiful screams!
They resound through our dreams
As she cries for the children she cherished.

The tale, often told, every Mexican knows;
they'll glance over their shoulders at night.
A coyote screams near. "La Llorona is here!"
It's repeated in justified fright.

Young and slender and fair,
she appears with wet hair,
with sable mantilla and gown;
Or she comes as a fey, "¡La vieja!" they say,
with shreds of a shroud hanging down.

She lures men to death.
When they feel her cold breath,
their strength simply leaves them, it's said;
For they follow and drown in the chill waters brown;
and she vanishes when they are dead.

They say it's just men who've abandoned women
seduced by their charms. How she languished!
And forever she wails on dim river trails
for the children she drowned in her anguish.

I'm told she attempted to save them too late.
She herself was drowned in the torrent.
The children are gone, but her ghost still wails on,
for her deed was so truly abhorrent.

Draw su serape tight if you travel at night!
Avoid river trails. ¡Escucharse!
What's that I hear? It's a woman's shriek near!
Could it be La Llorona? ¡Guardarse!

Glossary

¡Venga! - Come!
Compadre - friend, comrade
Adios a tu madre- Say goodbye to your mother
¡Cuidado! - Beware! Be careful
¡Que bonita mujer! - What a beautiful woman!
Muy triste - very sad
Fey - one forebodes death
La vieja - the old woman
Su serape - your shawl
¡Escucharse! - Hark! Listen!
Guardarse - Be on your guard!

---

1) Mexican parents sometimes warn their children to behave, lest La Llorona "get" them. ¡Ah, but La Llorona is no longer a threat to children; indeed, she regrets her act and weeps for her little ones! Logically, it is *men* who are in danger. After all, as is always the case where children are involved, there *was* a man in there somewhere!

2) All right. This author admits having made up the name of that river to rhyme with *Rio Grande.* Can you think of something better?

3) *Kak*: A type of saddle.

"She lures men to death . . ."

The next three poems are a triptych dealing with one of Arizona's most colorful characters. As they all concern prevarication and practical jokes, they are placed in this section: Legends, Lore, Myths and More.

Cyclone Bill's Big Windy

William Ellison (Abe) Beck had studied law in Texas. He worked in various places in Arizona Territory, and had arrived in Clifton by the early 1990s, where he himself became something of a local legend.[1]

"Madam, this is Cyclone Bill."
  The Miss her hand extended.
"Bill Beck!" I barked, and Judge Doan said,
  "Now, Will, don't be offended!

"As you're commonly known as Cyclone Bill,
  I thought *that* to proclaim."
"And *you're* commonly known as an S.O.B.
  Shall I call *you* by *that* name?"

Well, the lady up and sez to me
  ('twas a week or two ago),
"Why do they call you 'Cyclone Bill'?
  Now, I'd really like to know!"

Sez I, "Just out of law school,
  I thought I'd earn my glory
Convicting all the outlaws
  in this western territory

"Once the judge informed a rustler,
  'You've your rights and may expect
A court appointed counsel.
  I assign you William Beck,'

"He pointed straight at me, you see,
  as I sat there lookin' stilty.
The rustler squinted down and sez,
  'Your Honor, I plead guilty!'

"Well, that's the thing that ended
    my fine brief law career,
I left the bar, but 'twarn't too far
    to other bars quite near!

"With the S.P. building eastward,
    all them railroad supplies
Needed freightin' off to Tucson
    so it could materialize.

"A guy in Yuma's tellin' me
    'bout his fine big ten mule team—
'If the load gets through Apaches,
    why the rest will be a dream!

"'And if the driver makes it,
    me and him will sure be rich!'
So I signed on as his driver.
    Thought I'd try it for a hitch.

"Well, that Yuma feller noticed
    I'd been missin' more'n a year.
He'd heard rumors of wild Injuns.
    Couldn't find me anywhere!

"Run onto me in Tucson;
    wenta inquirin' 'bout his rig.
Seemed a trifle discomembered;
    claimed his loss was mighty big;

"Sez I, 'I'z out about a week,
    when Apaches up and struck!
They was whoopin', roarin', yellin',
    arrows flyin' thick as dust.

"'I'z whippin' on them stubborn mules;
    the sky grew dark and lowerin'
The wind commenced to blowin'!
    It was downright overpowerin'!

"'Them Injuns raised a cyclone
by circlin' me around—
Soon the gol-durn mules, the wagons, me,
and freight was whirlin' 'round!

"'Just then Ol' Nance, that lead mule,
come a-spinnin' into sight.
I leapt aboard, clung to her ears;
then things turned black as night!

"'Now talk about a twister!
I guess I'm the prototype.
The tornado kept on turnin'
till the earth was out of sight!

"'But I stuck right on ol' Nancy,
and I aimed her toward the sky,
And we rode that heavin' cyclone!
We was really flyin' high!

"'We just kept right on a-twistin',
till I thought we'd never stop;
But we clumb right up that funnel cloud,
and rode her to the top!

"'She bucked, she whirled, she crow-hopped;
she twirled us round and round
Till we'd plumb wore out that booger,
and we gently floated down

"'Way out in the midst of nowhere—
desert, sand. and dried up lakes.
Just me and Nance, and cactus plants,
and scorpions, and snakes.

"'Apaches gone! The cyclone too!
Then, suddenly as day,
A little ol' dust devil struck
and spun ol' Nance away!

"'The last time that I seen her,
she's a-headin' for the moon,
And her tail was just a floppin'
about half a ear past noon!

"I just walked in this direction
whence the twister it had came,
And I got here just this evenin'!
Now, that's how I got my name![2]

"It wuz just the way I told it!
It's the truth that I proclaim!
If you need a twister, sister,
well, ol' Cyclone Bill's the name!"[3]

---

1) The story appears in many sources. One is Banks, "*Odd and Bizarre People Make Historical Footnotes,*" *Rattlesnake Blues,* (Phoenix, 2000), p. 106.
2) Amazingly, some historians disagree with Bill's account of how he acquired his nickname! They contend that the ex-lawyer had knocked a man over the head with "the leg of a cow", causing the victim to feel like he had been "hit by a cyclone."
3) A play on words. "Twister" is a common term for "bronco buster." Bill is offering to break the lady's horses for her; he has just claimed that he rode the bucking cyclone *(twister)*, and is therefore, well qualified for the job.

"We just kept right on a-twistin'…"

Transformation Trick

William Beck was what would today be called physically challenged. After he gave up his law career, he had to make his way by his wits. He possessed a sharp mind and a wry sort of humor which made him popular in every community to which he ventured.

Cyclone Bill's left leg was shorter—
Good six inches less than right;
And one of Bill's most favorite stunts
Was enjoyed most any night
A new bartender came along
To whom Bill would be unknown,
And all his cronies loved to watch
This ruse of the ol' Cyclone:

He'd turn his hat 'round backwards,
Put his kerchief point up front,
Then, standin' on his short left leg
From end of the bar he'd grunt,
"Drinks on me—for the whole dang crowd!"
While drinks were being set up
He'd step around to the other end
And change his clowning get up:

He'd turn his scarf with tails to front,
His hat, turn back to backwards;
He'd stand up tall on his long right leg
And listen for the blunt words,
"Where the hell's that sawed off runt
That ordered all these drinks?
That short high-hatted varmint's gone!
"By gum, this really stinks!"

Unlikely Candidate

Ol' Bill was always playing pranks
on unsuspecting cronies
Till none were unsuspecting,
for they'd sampled Bill's baloney.
So several drinking buddies
without their pal's detection
Decided they would run Ol' Bill
in Clifton's next election.

Now, they got up a petition
and submitted it quite late:
A secret plan to make their man
a write-in candidate
For Clifton's *Justice of the Peace:*
Their pal in the position
To give incumbent, ol' Abe Boyles,
some hefty competition.

And when the votes were tallied up
and the jokesters had their fun,
It seems there was but little doubt,
ol' Cyclone Bill had won!
But as he'd been a write-in
for the J.P. category,
Boyles insisted on a checkup;
a recount was mandatory.

The election board got busy,
every write-in vote regarded,
And when their job was finished,
thirteen ballots were discarded.
Some votes were cast for *William Beck,*
and these they had retained,
But there was some disparity
'mongst those that still remained:

One vote for just plain *Cyclone,*
  eleven for *Cyclone Bill.*
One for *Tornado William;*
  Oh, it must have been a thrill
For Boyles to win by just three votes,
  But that proper politician;
Never heard the least complaint
  from his stalwart opposition.

Cry of the Death Bird

Written from the point of view of Dan Moore, as recounted in his Short Stories of the Southwest. Shades of E.A. Poe!

Wakened by the vi'lence raging,
Nature's forces battle waging,
We, routed from our bedground camp,
Stumbled up, all cold and damp.

So on a March night dark and dreary
Four tired hunters, spent and weary,
All fearful of the lightning's crack,
Had ridden horseback to a shack.

Deafened by the thunder crashing,
They found, by streaks of lighting flashing,
A wrecked and ruined miner's dwelling;
And thus my tale begins its telling.

Now, holding to the door's worn handle,
Old Jules Boudreoux lit a candle.
There revealed, by feeble glow,
A room abandoned long ago.

And, ah! We thought our fortune good—
Against the wall, a pile of wood!
From rusted hinges hung the door,
And gaping holes in the rotted floor

Attested to long years of aging.
Still, outside, the vi'lence raging
Made the old place seem inviting,
All, in chorus, now uniting,

Four voices cried out, "Let's go in!"
Now, somewhat shielded from the din,
We struck a flame in the fireplace.
As its warm glowing lit each face,

Every hunter chose his place
As far from hole in floor or roof
(The place was far from waterproof!)
As every hunter could discover—
Me, Dad, Jules, and my older brother.

I, a kid—soaked, tired and scared—
Was truly glad the men had dared
Ride out into the fearful storm,
For here I fell asleep quite warm!

As cheerful fire burned low and lower,
The howling wind swept 'round the door.
Around, above, and through, and under,
As lightning split the dark asunder.

Between the thunder claps exploding
There came a sound of grim foreboding:
A scream to chill and terrify!
"My God!" yelled Jules, "The death bird's cry!"

All of us knew the tale of old,
Which wise old women grimly told
Of bird that screeched it's prophesy:
"Death is near! So flee! So flee!"

"My God!" yelled Jules, "The death bird's cry!"

Four frightened hunters, but one thought:
To leave before death's dark onslaught!
"Lightning's sure to strike this shack!"
Cried Dad, as we raced, fearful, back—

Back into the dreadful night,
Out of rude room, warm and bright,
Into night—wet, cold and black.
Over shoulders glancing back,

Fully expecting a burst of flame
To light the night from whence we came.
Soon thunder'd ceased its awful roar,
No lightning flashes as before.

Then, gradually, the cold rain ceased,
A pale star shone in the graying east.
Old Jules declared, "Just up a piece"
Was a place to rest man, boy, and beast.

In the side of a cliff—a shallow cave.
The two men each a long sigh gave,
And, dropping on the hard rock floor,
Were soon asleep, as they'd been before.

But we two boys, though cold and tired,
Were curious as to what transpired
There, where we'd slept the night before.
Had a wolf come slinking through the door?

Had lightning set the shack on fire?
So then and there we did conspire,
And by first light of dawning day,
We ever so softly sneaked away.

Down to where our mounts were tied,
And then, how swiftly did we ride!
The cabin stood in light of morning.
So, what the import of the warning?

We laughed at the tale of the unseen bird
Whose spine-chilling shriek all four had heard.
We wondered on which limb he'd sat,
Convinced it had been some pant'er cat.*

"Hush! Listen! What's that noise?" Joe said.
Though leaves hung silent overhead,
A raspy rustling sound we heard.
Afraid by day? That seemed absurd!

But wait! The sound came from within.
"What's that?" my brother asked again.
We pushed aside the creaking door.
The fire had called from 'neath the floor
A hoard of reptiles warmed awake—
The place was crawling with rattlesnakes!

---

* *Pant'er cat:* panther or wild cat. Often pronounced "painter" in the south.

Kingman

Hardy pioneers crossed northern Arizona on the way to California, but were dismayed by the fierce winds of the high western deserts. This is the tale the locals tell about how their town became settled.

The leader said, "We'd best stop here
til that tarnal wind stops blowin'.
I think it might die down by dawn;
then we can keep on goin'."

So they all made camp, fixed supper,
got married, had children and died,
And that whole thing's still goin' on
up there—
Neither wind nor the town would subside,
I swear!
Folks have taken it all in their stride
up there,
Yes, Kingman is still goin' on!

(Story from Owen Finch, Kingman, Arizona)

Stilt Stock Stampede

This one is, obviously, a little more " lore" than the ones before, but it is based on an actual incident. It has been placed in this section only because of the fictionalized treatment I have given the tragic incident. It is dedicated to my good friends, the brothers Cook, who know about these things.[1]

I met a gal named Win-i-fred;
She was so sweet and pretty!
She said she'd been a *milliner*
Back East in New York City.

I asked her, "Wheat or oats?" She said,
"It's *hats*! You must know that!"
It really would have got my goat
And closed our little chat,

Except she slipped and dropped a tip
That went off like a light!
She said she needed *ostrich plumes*
To make her hats just right!

So I rented us a carriage,
For the ostrich ranch to ride;
But I sure did feel disparaged
(Cowboys ought to ride astride!)

Out on the range, I said, "It's strange,
The way them cows are built!"
Then I realized, with some surprise,
That stock was all on stilts!

I thought I'd steal a little smooch,
But that was quite a switch!
Did you ever get all puckered up
To find you'd kissed a *ostrich*?

We'd just arrived at the big bird ranch,
When I heard a dreadful sound!
Then all at onct we was amongst
The dust clouds blowin' round.

Dang well I knew, from how it blew,
We's right smack in the track
Of a sticky stiff stilt stock stampede
A frightful fowl attack!

There warn't no joy for this old boy!
I wondered how the dickens
I got fixed up to get mixed up
With them inflated chickens!

They was squawkin' and a-squallin',
And them stiff stick stilt stock legs
Was a-clawin' and a-pawin',
And the hens was layin' eggs!

I could see the wranglers clust'rin'
All a-pushin' for the lead—
Them famous *feather dustin'*
Buckaroos, a-gainin' speed![2]

Well, Sweet Thing started squealin',
And the whole thing was a blur
Of feathered things with necks and wings,
And buggy wheels, and her!

Then Win-i-fred stepped on my head
And jumped out of the rig.
I think I said, "I think I'm dead!"
But like a whirligig,

The buggy swung the other way,
And I could see quite plainly
That gal from New York City was
Outrunnin' them ungainly

Birds. Although I'd heard
They're the fastest things alive!
She's out front! They bore the brunt
Of the dust that she contrived!

Have you ever seen a lady
With her hat flowers disarranged,
And egg-yolk drippin' down from every rose?
Her veil a-trailin' feathers
As she gallops 'crost the plains,
A ostrich plume protrudin' from her nose?

Well, the last time that I seen her,
She was headin' up Four Peaks—
(All four at onct—that's quite a stunt!)
Now it's goin' on six weeks

Since that fowl wreck, but sure as heck,
If we ever get together,
There ain't no doubt, we won't go out
A huntin' ostrich feathers!

---

1) A buggy carrying a man and a woman actually overturned during an ostrich stampede in 1914. The woman was killed. The location of the accident was 59th Avenue (then called Lateral 18) and Lower Buckeye Road. (James E. Cook, letters to author, June, 1999 and 2002).

2) Reference to Dean Cook's inimitable song, "*The Feather Duster Cowboy*" in *Arizona Born* (Glendale, Arizona 1998), p. 51. (It's even better when Dean sings it!)

"Did you ever see a lady . . . as she gallops crost the plains . . .?

Hard to decide where to put this little gem of a story. It was given to me by Barb Baker of Show Low who swears that it's true, but due to its content I will include it in this section under the heading ". . . Myths and More." This one and the preceding poem are the "more."[1]

Swap Me A Biscuit

I used to do some guidin'
Down on the lower Blue,
And Fred Martin was the finest cook
I think I ever knew.

Why, when it come to trail herd stew,
(*Son of a* .... whatcha call it),[2]
Why I'd foller his chuck wagon
Just most any place he'd haul it!

His frijoles and his hash were great!
His dried apple pies, real fine!
(Claimed he crimped 'em with his old false teeth—
Cause that makes the best design!)

He fixed us "*hmmm, hmmm* in a sack",[3]
(Now that's puddin' made of suet.)
I reckon he's the only cook
I ever knew could do it!

When huntin' parties started out,
It was Fred they'd want for chuck,
And times we knew we'd get him,
Well, we figgered, "We're in luck!"

'Cause what he made the very best—
Either wood stove or Dutch oven—
Was biscuits! Watch that crew come up
Just a-pushin' and a-shovin'

To get to ol' Fred's biscuits,
Of which we could eat right smart!
We'd rustle up some kindlin' wood
To give Fred a good head start.

One time we's camped at HU-Bar,
We'd packed in seven miles
To that little old log cabin;
Fred had done swept out the piles

Of trash and stuff the rats had left;
The place was lookin' good.
When we got in, he's shovin' in
A few more sticks of wood

To that big ol' iron Mazda
And the room was smellin' great;
There's big thick steaks and chili beans,
Boy, we could hardly wait!

But Fred, he said we'd have to stall
For just a few more minutes,
"This oven just ain't heatin' right!"
And he kept peepin' in it.

"These biscuits, they ain't hardly browned!"
We kept hearin' that about 'em,
But we was starved and 'llowed as how
We'd have to eat without 'em.

Now, Fred just kept a-checkin'
And a lookin' kinda hurt;
He set out a pot of honey,
Said, "We'll have 'em for dessert!"

And when at last he set 'em on
That rough ol' wood plank table,
He thought we'd wolf 'em up real fast—
But none of us was able!

Why them things was hard as dornicks![4]
We laughed and Chuck said, "Shucks!
We could shoot 'em in our slingshots
And kill ourselves some bucks!"

Well, Fred, he was embarrassed,
Set the pan down on the floor,
And Slim took down that fiddle
That'd he'd hung up by the door.

Someone had brought *Jack Daniels*,
So we's drinkin' and a-smokin';
Just listenin' to the music,
A-visitin and jokin',

When Tuffy put his finger up
And motioned us for quiet.
He pointed us to look *that way*,
Oh, brother, what a riot!

There was utter total silence,
Nobody said a word,
For there was a great big *pack rat*
A-totin' a dried horse turd!

He didn't seem to see us,
All he was lookin' at
Was that pan of Fred's cold biscuits,
What a feast for one pack rat!

Then we busted right out laughin',
And I reckon that rat heard,
'Cause he up and grabbed a biscuit
And he left his dried horse turd!

Poor Fred. He really got it!
We could not contain our mirth.
Red said, "Fred, there goes one biscuit—
You can see what it was worth!"

But I tell you, that warn't nothin'!
Back that rat come to the shack;
Quick, he up and grabbed his horse turd,
And he put Fred's biscuit back!

---

1) Personal interview with Barbara Baker, June, 2000.

2 "Son-of-a-bitch stew" or simply "son-of-a-bitch" (sometimes called "son-of-a-gun" in polite company). It was made of sweet breads, marrow gut, and kidneys, which were added to the best of the calf meat.

3) "*Hmmm, hmmm* in a sack": Bastard in a sack.

4) *Dornicks*: (Gaelic) rocks, especially field stones turned up by a plow.

"He put Fred's biscuit back . . ."

V. 20th Century

"The century on which we are entering can be and must be the century of the common man."

— Henry Wallace, 1942

"So gladly, from the songs of modern speech, men turn and see the stars and feel the free shrill wind."

— Andrew Lang

Battle Ground

The incident described in this poem took place in October 1901, after the Smith gang had killed two young posse men in March.)

Things had gotten out of hand;
Bill Smith's ornery outlaw band[1]
were holed up on the land down on the Black.
Henry Barrett and Bill Phelps
Had lost cattle to those whelps,
and both had sworn they'd get their cattle back!

Autumn nights were growing chill;
Heading south near Springerville,
a herd of stolen cattle was observed.
Leaves were turning orange and red
When twenty-five or thirty head,
were reported to be headed down the curve.

Now the ranchers, growing bolder,
(Though the nights got cold and colder:
from September to October—skiffs of snow),
A vigilante posse formed.
Ignoring threats of fearful storms,
they gathered on the range above Show Low.

Sharp and Peterson joined Barrett;[2]
They had all agreed to share it
if the bounty for the outlaws they received.
The Maxwell brothers Bill and Arch,
As trackers, now, they joined the march,
Crosby and Holgate, too, would hunt the thieves.[3]

The Maxwell boys were expert scouts;
The ranchers hadn't any doubt
they could lead them to those rustlers in the hills.
So they headed toward the rim,
Someone whistling a hymn.
All depended on the Maxwells' tracking skills.

Loyal to their ranger code
    Arizona Rangers rode[4]
To join the rancher's posse up at Greer,
    little knowing that tonight
Would see the first big Ranger fight.
    The riders of the posse then appeared.

Near New Mexico's state line
    the trailing posse found the sign
Near Dead Man's Crossing
    where the rustlers camped.
They followed south past Slaughter's ranch.
The posse knew they'd get their chance.
    'midst juniper and piñon, oak and pine.

As they neared the outlaws' campsite,
    sunset's gold and crimson lamplight
Cast shadows 'mongst the canyon's walls and trees.
    The posse then and there dismounted;
Their excitement now surmounted
    all the fears that rode the chilling autumn breeze.

As they cautiously drew near,
Three quick shots rang loud and clear,
    and every man could hear the echoes ringing.
All the horses gave a start.
    Panic rose in every heart,
The unexpected shots, dark terror bringing.

But the shots were not repeated,
    and they wouldn't be defeated,
So the posse pressed on forward toward the quarry.
Drops of blood upon the snow.
    Slow, deliberate, they go.
    Quiet. Cautious. Vigilant and wary.

In a deep and narrow canyon,
    Rustler Smith and his companions
Were gathered round the bear
    which they'd just shot.
Evening light was growing dim,
    and the posse on the rim
Could see the rustlers moving round the spot.

Trampling down the frozen ground,
all the outlaws gathered round,
While dressing out the bear by sunset's glow.
Tried to beat approaching dark;
when their dogs began to bark,
For the posse'd tracked the bear's blood
through the snow.

Carlos Tafolla and Duane Hamblin
with their very lives were gamblin';
They stood, with young Bill Maxwell, in a clearing.
Moved out front, while all the others
their advance expertly covered,
quite suddenly, the rustlers disappearing.

With his Spanish Mauser ready,
Barrett called, "Look out!" and Steady!"
To the three men in the valley down below.
Heeding Barrett's admonition,
Hamblin fell to prone position;
but the others? Perfect targets 'gainst the snow!

Tafolla ordered the offenders
to step forward and surrender.
Long silence, then Bill Smith walked slowly out,
The baited, quiet desperation
of their present situation,
Shared by hunter, hunted, ranger, dog, and scout.

Bill Smith didn't aim to trifle—
Came out draggin' that old rifle,
and everyone aghast at his appearing.
Then Smith, suddenly grown bolder,
Swung the rifle to his shoulder;
All hell broke loose right out there in the clearing.

Maxwell then and there was slain,
took three bullets to the brain;
Tafolla, badly wounded, went on firing.
Oh, the rifle shots flew hot;
killed a hound dog on the spot,
but the posse and the outlaws seemed untiring.

As the acrid, white smoke swirled,
  shadows closed upon the world,
And the rustlers, in the darkness, all survived.
Tafolla, calling out for water,
  died, completing that day's slaughter.
  Thus, two law abiding gunmen lost their lives.

It's still talked about today,
  how the outlaws got away,[5]
While the ranger and the scout, with dog and bear
  lay there in the bloody snow.
The posse talked of who would go
  and tell Tafolla's wife of the affair.

There was not a member that
  would touch Bill Maxwell's hat, [6]
Stained dark with Bill's own blood.
There was no sound.
Man and beast's blood on the snow
  in the day's dim afterglow
And that spot is still today
  called *Battle Ground.*[7]

---

1) Two of the gang were Bill Smith's younger brothers Al and George.
2) Ranchers Hank Sharp and Pete Peterson.
3) Ranchers Elijah Holgate and Lorenzo Crosby.
4) Governor Nathan Oakes Murphy created the Arizona Rangers August 30, 1901. He appointed Burt Mossman, former Superintendent of the vast Aztec Land and Cattle Company (Hash Knife), as Captain.
5) The outlaws were never apprehended, but were chased out of Arizona. Smith sent several messages to the mother of Bill Maxwell, expressing his regret at having killed her son and stating that he didn't know his opponent was Maxwell. Smith also wrote a detailed letter to Burt Mossman, head of the Arizona Rangers, explaining the events of October 8th. Smith's mother claimed that he and his brothers had fled to Argentina.
6) The hat, with the crown blown out of it, is said to have lain undisturbed for years. Perhaps it was finally dragged off by some animal.
7) Many sources. One of the best: Bill O'Neal, *The Arizona Rangers* (Austin, TX, 1987), pp. 12-16.

Lady in the Copper Mesh Gown

Sharlot Mabridth Hall's existence spanned the turning of two centuries. I have included it in the 20th Century section because it was in the latter part of her life that Miss Sharlot's two great goals became reality: Arizona was admitted to the union as the forty-eighth state on February 14, 1912 and the Sharlot Hall Museum opened its doors at Prescott in 1928.

Sharlot was a prairie girl reared on a Kansas farm.
No friends save her mother—
and later the brother
who up and came along.

James Hall, like many farmers,
felt a woman's place in life
Was cooking and cleaning—not reading or dreaming
except for his own sweet wife.

Adeline he respected,
and he did not interfere
When she taught their daughter to read and write—
though he thought it slightly queer.

The home had two books only—
Mother made no apology
For being so few, they just had to do—
Mesmerism and *Phrenology*.

Then arrived a stranger on that barren Kansas plain.
Folks thought him quite odd—but to Sharlot, a god
had stepped into her world to reign!
They gave him odd looks—
for he owned lots of books,

And "Who walks about by themselves?"
Sharlot set out to meet him;
and one day did greet him.
Soon she stood before his tall shelves.

Now her world stretched beyond
the chasm that yawned
Past that farthest horizon line:
History, philosophy, art and biography,
all suited this eight year old fine!

But her folks Kansas left, they headed out West
for that brand new territory—
This place, *Arizona,* with its diverse persona,
And so continues our story.

When her dad took to mining,
young Sharlot was shining
As cook and the guard of the gold.
The while, unsuspecting, she started collecting
artifacts from the past, we are told.

She helped on the ranch, her heart on the branch
O'er the sweet springs of creativity.
A typewriter won, and thus was begun
a life full of great activity.

This Kansas farm girl found her heart in a whirl,
truly charmed by the rugged Southwest.
The rough land did need her,
and as a strong leader,
young Sharlot was one of the best!

She wrote poems and stories in such categories
as pioneers, Indians and miners,
Of white, brown, and red—people living and dead.
She sold them and basked in the glory!

Yes, editors noticed and purchased her work
and gave her the space she deserved
To sing the land's praises in rich glowing phrases—
Arizona's sweet singing bird.

She sought ruins and mines,
through cactus and pine,
Over mountains and reservations
seeking the facts and old artifacts
to assure their own preservation.

Of course there were those
who looked down their nose:
"Imagine that woman! Such brass!
Out riding with *men!* Why, she should have been
at home like *all* women of class!"

"She's taking a trip to the far northern Strip!"[1]
And, well, that contention was true.
Caring not if it surfaced,
she accomplished her purpose—
Research for a project in view.

My, how she opposed that new bill proposed![2]
Couched in words so grandiose
'Twould end all the glory of her dear territory
It's intent now darkly disclosed:

New Mexico reunited! it's cry.
Dissolve the new territory!
Sharlot sprang to the fore, crying,
"No! Nevermore!"
She'd proclaim Arizona's own story!

So she traveled and spoke,
for she knew 'twas no joke,
To United States Congress, no jest.
Little cared they for the people's dismay—
that sparse population out west.

Her efforts won out, for there is no doubt
the Senators' minds she impressed;
For day, great and glorious, found Sharlot victorious!
Her efforts had stood to the test.[3]

And after that fight she continued to write
of the early day pioneers;
Of ancient ones' dwellings, hieroglyphics compelling
on the cliffs of the canyons out here.

How grand she would be when she went to D.C.
as a presidential elector.
In her copper mesh gown, the toast of the town!,
All of Washington came to respect her.[4]

This western land, vast, gained statehood at last,
with Sharlot its worthy historian!
She loved pretty clothes and often wore those
with a charm completely Victorian.

Calvin Coolidge, they say, was bewitched by this gay
intelligent, charming elector.
Why, some say he *smiled* and *talked* quite awhile—
and behaved like the lady's protector![5]

In Yavapai County, she acquired and restored
The log house at the foot of the hill.
There her soul must reside, for her spirit presides
in the "Governor's Mansion" there still.

To her credit and fame, the place bears her name;
The museum is called *Sharlot Hall.*
And there still abide those things which with pride
she acquired and kept for us all.

Artifacts she collected are rightly respected,
From the ancients and miners reclaimed;
From governmental persona who led Arizona,
back when Prescott knew capital fame.[6]

Sharlot has told us that life is a game,
the poker cards marked before dealing;
With chips on the table, the lady is able
to laugh! It resounds from the ceiling.[7]

Miss Sharlot, creator of *Cactus and Pine*,[8]
We, of old Arizona's rough sod,
Lift high the glass to toast you at last,
And commend your sweet soul up to God.[9]

---

1) *The Arizona Strip*: That section of Arizona which lies north and west of the Colorado River. Due to the enormity of the Grand Canyon, the Strip is remote and far more accessible to Utah than to Arizona.
2) The Hamilton Bill would have rejoined the two territories of New Mexico and Arizona, and thus, would have brought them into the union as a single state.

3) New Mexico and Arizona were admitted to the union as separate states just a week apart, New Mexico on January 6 and Arizona on February 14, 1912. (It was thus called *the Valentine State* and *the Baby State* for many years).
4) Sharlot went to Washington as a presidential elector for Calvin Coolidge in January, 1925. Her gown was made for her by an Arizona copper company and was accompanied by a matching purse and hat, the latter decorated with representations of cactus. Miss Sharlot was the toast of the nation's capitol. Her picture appeared in most major American newspapers.
5) Coolidge was reputed to be a man of few words. His detractors called him "Silent Cal".
6) Prescott was the first territorial capital (1864); Tucson became capital in 1867.
7) *O, Life is a game of poker,*
   And I've played it straight to the end;
   But the last chip's down on the table,
   And I'm done with the game, my friend.
   . . . Sharlot Hall, "*Cash In*," *Cactus and Pine*, p. 231.
8) Sharlot Hall died April 9, 1943. Most complete source consulted: Dorothy Daniels Anderson, *Arizona Legends and Lore: Tales of Southwestern Pioneers*, pp. 27-51.
9) *Cactus and Pine* is the title of one collection of Sharlot's poetry (Prescott, 1989).

From a photograph in Sharlot Hall Museum Archives, Prescott, Arizona.

Sharlot Hall with her Blickensdeerfer typewriter

A Sojourner's Luck

The La Fortuna Mine near Yuma in Arizona Territory was discovered in 1893. Chinese who came to the area to make money to be sent back to the old country (rather than establish permanent residence) were called "Sojourners". They were at the bottom of the social ladder of the frontier; hence, this incident, which occurred in 1903, is somewhat remarkable. (The attempt at Chinese dialect in this poem is in no way intended in disrespect of the Chinese people).

Charlie Sam was a sojourner
from some land across the ocean.
He'd arrived to seek his fortune
at the La Fortuna Mine.
A boarding house he opened,
worked and tended with devotion
His rooms were dark and crowded,
but they say the food was fine!

Al Eaton ran the gambling hall
and saloon where Charlie squandered
A good bit of that fortune
he had come so far to make.
Just as sure as Charlie's pig tail
would be hanging way back yonder,
He'd be there each Friday evening,
rich or poor, his chance to take.

One evening Charlie's luck was bad.
The cards all fell against him.
Lost the last cent of his money
so he staked his boardinghouse.
Vowed he'd win or lose his fortune,
But luck never recompensed him,
Without curse or look of anger,
he rose, quiet as a mouse.

Facing Al, Sam said, "It rate now,
    soon the day shrift, they be waking.
You must go and stalt the bleakfast,
    you must set the bled to lize."
Al said, "Shoot! I ain't no cosi![1]
    Don't just stand there verbalizing!
You start breakfast! It's *your* kitchen.
    Go on! Make some apple pies!"

It wasn't long till gambler's luck
    swung to Oriental will, then
Charlie cleaned out all Al's pockets
    and he won the whole saloon.
Charlie quietly went over,
    and he cleaned out all the till, then
"I no dlink, no sell no whiskey."
    You take brack youl own saroon!" [2]

---

1) *Cosi*: short for *cocinero* (cook). Usually pronounced *coosie*.
2) Ruth Conner, "*Charlie Sam and the Sojourners*," *The Journal of Arizona History* XIV:4 (Winter 1973), pp. 303-304.

The Ballad of George Manly

A vignette from That Cowboy From Burro Creek by Grace Neal (Kingman, 1991), p. 71.

Come all you bold young cowboys,
 a story I'll relate
About when Arizony
 was a young and restless state.

South of the Arizony Strip
 where pine trees touch the sky
Lie the lower hills and valleys
 called the land of the Walapai.
(Sad are the songs the wild wind sings
 in the land of the Walapai).[1]

'Twas in Mohave County
 where the Music Mountains spring;
In cedar, sage, and grama grass,
 the wind its wild songs sing.

In '22 or '23 my story shall begin,
 when a cowboy named George Manly
Came proudly riding in—
 to the ranch of John and Amy Neal.[2]
 John said, "Just start right in!"

He knew George to be trustworthy,
 for he'd hired the lad before—
A cheerful, carefree cowboy
 who could handle every chore;

And now he was returning,
 his face alight with pride,
For close behind, on a small bay mare,
 rode the cowboy's new young bride.

True to his word, returning
for the roundup in the Spring,
The shouts of his companions
from corral and bunkhouse ring.

The Neals are most obliging,
and they gladly hire him on,
And they welcome George's sweet young wife,
the ranch to live upon.

It wasn't long thereafter,
when the irrigation flowed,
John sent George up 'long the ditch,
the water gates to close.

The day dragged on, increasing hot,
and George had not returned;
John sent his son and nephew, then,
the reason to be learned.

The boys approached the water gate,
as the sun was sinking low,
The sky was burnished copper
with a reddish golden glow.

As they rounded that last sagebrush,
where the floodgate was concealed,
A fearful cry rang from the boys
at what was there revealed:

The water flowed on steadily,
with soothing swish and splash,
While the cowboy's blood, as readily,
flowed from a ragged gash

That split across his fine young throat.
The final sound he heard
Must have been the water singing
its somber deathly dirge.

The kids stood frozen in their tracks;
they dared advance no farther,
For George's dog Amigo,
his master watching over,

Stood bristling there and snarling,
lest anyone come near;
The boys fled back along the track—
two swift and frightened deer.

The children slid into the ranch,
hysterical and screaming,
"George is dead!" they stammered.
Amy thought they must be dreaming,

But the cowboys leapt as one to horse,
and off the party sped
To see if this sad tale were true;
their young companion, dead?

Swiftly came the rancher, then,
along with all his crew;
Their calloused hands were trembling
as their horses fairly flew.

The thunder of their hoof beats
blocked every other sound,
For in their hearts all were afraid
the young cowboy had drowned.

And when they came upon the place,
the cow dog ceased to growl,
For he knew these were his master's friends.
Each wore a dreadful scowl.

Ringed close around the body then,
their horses panting, tired,
They stood in silence pondering
Just what had there transpired.

Had the dog turned on his master
to inflict that ghastly wound?
Fled some cutthroat silhouetted
against the rising moon?

Then every one dismounted
and compared the signs they found:
The swelling of the body and
the marks upon the ground.

Then George's friends conjectured
that despite the bloody lake,
The cowboy George, their partner,
had been bit by a rattlesnake.

The dog had sprung to rescue,
but, alas, had come too late,
The rattler'd struck George in the throat,
as he knelt to close the gate.

Amigo'd killed the hateful snake;
it lay dead among the weeds,
All punctured by the dog's fierce fangs,
there in the blood stained reeds.

So the cowboys all discussed it
and agreed, beyond a doubt,
George plunged his knife in his own throat
to let the poison out!

Then, riding up, his fair young wife
came upon this frightful scene;
the mighty wolf would shudder
had he heard her fearful scream!

Mounted on a misty mustang
with stars in the mane and tail.
George, soundlessly as his horse's feet,
rode that ascending trail,
As a merciful stream hid a woman's screams
and Amigo's mournful wail.

Think kindly on George Manly,
for his violent death was strange.
He met his fate by a water gate
on an Arizony range.

My story has a moral—which
 I now reveal to you:
If you be one of those wild young bucks
 who would be a buckaroo:

Remember poor George Manly,
 if you're lookin' for romance.
Think twice before you head out West
 to an Arizony ranch!

---

1) The official spelling of this Indian tribe was later changed by the U.S. Government to *Hualapai* (sometimes appearing *Hualpai)*; however, the mountains in northwestern Arizona, and many of these Native Americans themselves, retain the original spelling, *Walapai*. (The author recalls that Indian men on the baseball team at Frazier Wells wore caps with the letter "W" for Walapai).

2) This tragedy took place on the ranch of Grace Neal's in-laws, the parents of her husband Leonard, where she and Leonard lived until 1928 when they moved to Cane Springs Ranch.

Mogollon Mountain Moonshine

During prohibition years, the mountainous area of the rim country afforded excellent cover for moonshiners. Italicized quotations in the poem actually appeared in newspapers of the time. Many thanks to James E. Cook for this good story.[1]

Up in northern Gila County,
where the hunters shoot for bounty,
It's mighty far from anyplace, you know.
Why, the only way of gettin' there
Risks life and limb, I do declare!
"*Foller the ruts*"—the only way to go!

Well, the place is known for moonshine,
Unadulterated moonshine![2]
(Gun powder mixed, I think, with turpentine).
But ruts, especially when it's rainin',
has our customers complainin'.
If we could build a road, that would be fine!

"Somebody's got to go to Globe.
To try to get a decent road!"
(Globe's the county seat with Gila's mother lode);[3]
Well, the Judge, that durned old dunderhead—
Whose face looks like a thunderhead;
Said, "*What you need's a* pipeline, *not a road!*"

---

1) The 18th Amendment to the U.S. Constitution, passed in 1917, established prohibition throughout the country. Prohibition was repealed by Amendment 21, which returned the liquor problem to the individual states in 1933.
2) In Rim Country, moonshine was often made from maguey (agave). Plant heads and water were the only ingredients—hence these stillers were actually making tequila. The head of the plant is sweet like sugar cane, so additional sugar is not required.
3) Globe was a copper mining community.

"What you need's a pipeline . . ."

Down on the Blue

The Blue River meanders through eastern Arizona, near the New Mexico border. There one can find a community by the name of Blue. Locals refer to the whole region as "Down on the Blue."

Jes Burke, he was a mountain man,
  Who lived "down on the Blue";
He liked to eat about as well
  As anyone I knew.

His wife said bread and gravy was
  His favorite thing to eat.
Old Jes, he said, "She makes good bread,
  And her gravy can't be beat!"

Jes Burke, lived up "Down on the Blue,"
  His hair was dark and wavy,
Said, "If I had ten acres, I
  Would plant it all in gravy!"

From Betty Chambliss Grammer's tale about Jes Burke in *Down on the Blue: Blue River, 1878-1986*, ed. Cleo Cosper Coor (Goodyear, 1992), p. 24.

Old Soup Bone

The Great Depression wasn't so great! One old bachelor explains.

There's certain thangs a feller
just hadn't ought to loan!
Case in point: I'm tellin' y'all
about my good soup bone.

I got on with this guy o.k.,
till I loaned him mine one sprang,
He cooked her up with black eyed peas,
and ruint the dad-burn thang![1]

A Comment on the "Old Soup Bone"

By my "hillbilly poet" friend Jack Burdette[2]

Why, I plumb lost respect for him,
'cause, any idiot, see,
Knows for peas, you shouldn't use a bone,
use a slab of sow belly!

---

1) "I had a friend I got on with until I loaned him my soup bone. He went and cooked black-eyed peas with it and ruined it." (Margaret Shellabarger Axtell in Louis DeWald's *Arizona Highways Heritage Cook Book, pp 22.)*
2) As everyone knows, hillbillies whittle sticks and make moonshine in their spare time. Jack designs steel mills. Oh, well, there's apt to be an odd pup in every litter!

"They'll Know Who I Am!"

This tale was told by rancher Frank Chapman of Young, Arizona.

We was down in Pleasant Valley
  Hangin' round the rodeo,
When we seen a sight to pop your eyes!
  A thing we didn't know

Could happen in that country;
  Why, much to our surprise,
We seen a *airplane* comin'!
  We just stood there mesmerized.

It was settlin' in the pasture;
  The red dust really rolled!
We all rushed out to see that thang,
  And what did we behold

But a orange and yaller biplane,
  And painted purple on the side
Was a big mean lookin' bronco
  With a mustached dude astride.

And underneath, real fancy,
  Was these words, for all to see,
"*They'll know who I am!*" it said,
  As plain as it could be.

Pilot had a yaller kerchief,
  And a fringed and sequined shirt;
His pants was tucked into his boots,
  And he sure did like to flirt!

Blonde mustache, waxed and sharpened;
High peaked Montana hat.
Them pants was *ridin' britches;*
Stumpy sez, "Dang! Look at that!"

We all was wearin' Levi's,
Faded shirts that needed mends.
That dude looked a unfurled peacock
In a yard of speckled hens.

Soon we seen that yaller kerchief
Down around chute number three.
As he didn't look familiar,
Thought we'd see who he might be.

Then old Sam, upon the bull horn,
Like the voice of God exclaimed,
"Rider, number twenty-seven,
We didn't get your name!"

Ol' Ridin' Britches hollered back
Might nigh as loud as Sam,
"Just listen good, announcer!
The crowd *will tell you who I am!"*

Then he turned to us ol' punchers,
Us four poor ol' speckled hens,
Said, *"Yeah, when I make my ride, boys.*
They'll all *know who I am!"*

If he didn't want to tell his name,
We didn't give a damn,
But the way he said it rubbed us wrong,
That *"They'll know who I am!"*

"Rider number twenty-seven
Chute three on Greasy Grey!"
Jake slipped the bar; they busted out
Like a match throwed in dry hay.

That grey pitched and whirled and sunfished!
That ride was sure a bust!
Ol' *Britches* lit right on his head
And wallered in the dust.

Why, he didn't even brush off dirt;
just took off on the lam.
We watched him go—and we still don't know
just *who* the heck *he am!*

"We watched him go, And we still don't know . . ."

Two Old Hash Knife Cowboys

Most of the Hash Knife were good guys;
'Twas them as were out on the dodge
Built Hash Knife's rough reputation;
But two of them started the Lodge:[1]

Dick Grigsby—from 'round Adamana
and Johnny Paulsell partnered up
When age had precluded their riding,
And I was a little ol' pup

'Way out at the Petrified Forest.
Those old cowboys were really a sight—
Selling pop and petrified bookends
Yeah, those two old guys were all right!

They still wore the handlebar mustache—
Dick's was gray and Johnny's was white—
And high crowned uncreased flat-brimmed Stetsons.
They were honest and kind and upright.

"Uncle Johnny" and "Uncle Dick" Grigsby:
Two finer old gents never breathed.
They ran the place till the end of their days,
And both were sure nice to me![2]

---

1) This poem is lovingly dedicated to those two old Hash Knife cowboys Dick Grigsby and Johnny Paulsell. They furnished me with many a soda pop at the Rainbow Forest Lodge at the south end of the road through the Petrified Forest. (Headquarters is now at the north end of the Forest). Johnny had homesteaded a place out on the Milky Wash which, by the time of my arrival, had been transferred to his son Pat. (See next poem, *Buckaroo Waltz*.)

2) These two old gents were good to all the children, but I knew I got more than my share of attention. Uncle Dick often asked me to sing cowboy songs for him, and so we spent many an hour on the front porch of the lodge singing—and discussing the temperature and his trumpet vines, of which he was very proud. Much later I learned that he had explained his kindness to me with these words: "Poor little devil; she ain't got no mama".

Uncle Dick Grigsby

The Buckaroo Waltz

A song containing a bit of personal history from the author's youth at the Petrified Forest. It is dedicated to Pat and Juanita Paulsell, in deep appreciation for many an evening of fun.

Up at the school house or down at the lodge,
We'd tie up our ponies right by that old Dodge
That Pat and Juanita drove in from the ranch
Way out on the Milky to play for the dance.

With fiddle and guitar they'd do it up right;
Then swap back and forth for the rest of the night,
And I always thought those two should be blessed
For bringin' so many so much happiness.

We'd sprinkle cornmeal all over the floor,
Dance every dance and be beggin' for more,
With no thought of drinkin' or time for romance,
Just loving to twirl at an old cowboy dance.

Dance to the Buckaroo Waltz;
glide cross the floor in the lamplight.
Sway while the soft fiddles play;
who could forget those sweet nights?
We'd dance the polka, the Versouviene,
schottisches, two steps, La Rospa;
Then start all over again,
and end with the Buckaroo Waltz.

Often on nights when there wasn't a dance,
We country kids would just take every chance
To sing and to dance and to holler and laugh;
We'd pack the Victrola windup phonograph.

We'd take us some pop and the records we'd grab,
Then head us on out to that crumbling slab
Of concrete that out in the desert still lay—
The floor of a building from some by-gone day.

Then, how we would dance
While the moon shone up there,
Wearin' our boots out on that concrete square
To all the same tunes that our fiddlers knew:
Silver Bells, La Luz, and Waltz *Buckaroo.*

Dance to the Buckaroo Waltz;
  under the wide sky by starlight.
Sway while the soft fiddles play;
  who could forget those sweet nights?
We'd dance the polka, and Versouviene,
  schottisches, two steps, La Rospa;
Then start all over again,
  and end with the Buckaroo Waltz.

Journey to Turquoise Waters

The Havasupai Indians have, for several centuries, lived at the bottom of lower Grand Canyon. My Grandfather, Roy Hoovler, took the first water pipe into Havasupai Canyon on horseback in the late nineteen twenties or early thirties.[1]

I stood by the turquoise waters[2]
Where, despite the encumbrance of years,
I was keeping a date, albeit quite late,
With Granddad—'midst mist, time, and tears.
Having traversed the trail down the canyon,
I, surrounded by red ocher walls,
Was transfixed in that place,
with the spray in my face.
No sound, save the roar of the falls.

High above me, the waters divided,
Then violent, yet graceful, flowed there,
Falling frothy, like lace, down the great granite face,
An old woman's wayward white hair.[3]
Her voice rumbled deep in her bosom,
Majestic, compelling, complete,
And her aqua blue gown cascaded on down
And lay in a pool at her feet.

Many years have gone by since my Granddad
Rode his horse into the abyss
And, standing in spray this very same way,
Felt the canyon's gentle sweet kiss.
As a child, I promised him—someday,
Sometime in my life I would go
Down the same rocky trail,
where the coyotes still wail,
In the moonlight's dim ghostly glow.

So I've kept that date with my Granddad
Nearly sixty long years past the time
When I promised I'd go. Walking steady and slow,
Surely I hear his horse as I climb
Back out—up the trail of the canyon
Those hooves echo soft as new day.
There! Distant and dim—high above the dark rim—
It's before me each step of the way.

---

1) *Havasupai* (People of the turquoise waters): Ha (water), vasu (blue-green), pai (people). The Havasupai live "in Cataract Canyon, a great gash in the center of the immense plateau that drain(s) (sic) toward the Grand Canyon of the Colorado. Here, at a depth of 2,500 ft. they dug ditches and tilled and irrigated fields . . . about five to seven miles south of the Grand Canyon." ("*General Crook Visits the Supais*" ed. Frank E. Casanova, *Arizona and the West* [Autumn 1968].) There are about 600 Havasupai living in the canyon today. As a child I lived at Frazier Wells (or Frazier's Well) on the Hualapai (Pine Tree People) Reservation, only a few miles from Havasupai Canyon trail head; yet it was fifty-seven years before I made the hike to "The Land of the Turquoise Waters," which my grandfather had so highly praised.
2) The waters of the canyon are a beautiful turquoise color, but not from the high concentration of travertine in the water, as is commonly believed. Dr. Robert S. Gray, professor of geology at Santa Barbara City College states, "What would make the waters green/blue, and maybe even make the travertine look green, would be the algae. . . . These algae would . . . be aided by other living plants that might add to the coloring effect. . . . An important additional input is the sunlight being transmitted into the 'pools' along the creek. As the light penetrates into the water, it will be scattered by the water molecules as well as being absorbed. The deeper the pools, the more back-scattering will give a bluish color similar to the ocean's blue." This water is not drinkable, but the canyon does have a few fresh water springs, and the turquoise pools are delightful for swimming.
3) Floods cause drastic changes in the canyon. Havasupai Falls, one of four impressive waterfalls between the village and the river, presently drops in two long "braids" on either side of a huge stone "face" high above the placid blue-green pools below.

VI. Performance Cuts

Should you wish to learn any of the following fairly long poems, I suggest that you use the following cuttings. Thank you for acknowledging the author.

Belle of the Bar
Climax Jim
Rhyming Robber
Swap Me a Biscuit
Vigilante Coming

Belle of the Bar (Performance Cut)

For historical notes on this poem, see uncut version in section III.

'Twas a cold dark night in Prescott, January '98,
The place quite populated for a Monday night so late,
The bar and tables crowded, the room all thick with smoke.
The smell of men and liquor was enough to make one choke.

Yes, the place was a din; a veiled woman walked in;
Frank Williams, the barkeep, was stunned,
For she lifted her bundle up onto the bar
And took off in a fast limping run.

Well, it didn't take long to disrupt the place;
Abruptly, the very air changed!
Frank pulled back the cover, there to discover
A baby! How shocking and strange!

A brief heavy hush. Then all the men rushed
And pressed toward that end of the bar,
The miners, and ranchers, the railroaders came—
All those who most usually are

The drinkers and gamblers on tough Whiskey Row.
In such rugged and rough atmosphere
Of vice-filled saloons, full with smoke and spittoons,
Could an innocent angel appear?

The boys in the back room came hurrying out
Just as Frank was conscripted to read
The note that he'd found in the cloth wrapped around
The baby; and so he proceeds:

"'*This little baby belongs to John Bell,*
Give her to him, or call the law.
The woman who cared for her's down awful sick;
She can't do it no more.' Boys, that's all!"

John Bell had been known to frequent that place,
But he hadn't been seen for awhile;
And nobody offered to go look him up,
Each face was just lit by a smile.

Then somebody hollered, "Let's gamble for her!
Each toss of the dice is ten bucks!"
And so, 'twas agreed; it was something indeed,
More than forty men trying their luck!

It took quite awhile, a frown followed a smile,
As a high score was beat, "Man alive!"
Frank proclaimed we were done
And announced Bob had won:
"Full house! Three sixes, two fives!"

But as the old bachelor stepped up for his prize,
A man entered, all covered with snow.
Bob Groom was denied; Judge Hicks had arrived
And announced, "Boys, I'll have the last throw!"

They gave him the can, and every last man
Heard the rattle and roll of the dice.
Five sixes! He'd won! The old son-of-a-gun!
(Some claim that the dice rolled too nice).

Bob was unreconciled, but the judge got the child,
And took her straight home to his wife.
And many inquired as to what there transpired—
Most explaining he'd done in his life!

Now some people say that they named the girl *Chance,*
Because of the way Hicks acquired her,
But in fact, it was *Violet* he chose for her name,
And he loved her as if he had sired her.

But most people still call her Sweet Baby Bell,
She is known thus at home and afar.
For those who were there on that cold winter's night
Proclaimed her the *Belle of the Bar!*

Climax Jim: "My Favorite Outlaw" (Performance Cut)

For historical notes on this poem, see uncut version in Section II.

Jim entered the cattle business;
With a ranch, he was not encumbered.
He rustled all of his stock, they say,
his total take was unnumbered.

Now, Jim was so good with a running iron,
it seemed no brand could dissuade him,
So no one could prove he broke the law,
and no jail could blockade him.

"Most slippery bird in the whole southwest,"
said the Solomonville newspaper.
Of all the slipperies, Jim was best
Arizona's top escaper!

At picking locks, Jim surely was
the undisputed master.
Were there a test, he'd have proved the best
and would have done it faster.

When back at his job as "cattle boss,"
a wide loop Jim would swing,
Then, due to his art with a running iron,
no one could prove a thing!

He sold a dozen stolen steers
to the company butcher shop
At Clifton, then altered the payment check
so that he would come out on top.

As the law couldn't prove he was rustling,
they arrested him for check kiting,
And the prosecution produced the note;
so what was the use of Jim fighting?

Pronouncing the check as "Exhibit A",
the voice of the prosecution
Said, "Climax can't escape this time!
He must face his retribution!"

Jim whispered, to his attorney "Object!"
The young lawyer loudly objected!
The two counsels clashed vociferously;
the defendant seemed quite unaffected.

In all the commotion, Jim took a chew
and no one so much as eyed him,
Nor saw him lay the wet plug down
on the table there beside him—

On top of foresaid, "Exhibit A",
the check placed there for viewing.
"Order!" The judge's gavel fell,
and Jim sat calmly chewing.

Jim spat his wad in the handy spittoon,
and nobody saw what followed.
it seems he took a second chaw;
and no one noticed—-he swallowed.

The check and the plaintiff's case were gone,
and for this incompetence,
The judge pronounced the case dismissed—
for lack of evidence.

The Rhyming Robber (Performance Cut)

For historical notes on this poem, see uncut version in Section II

McNeil was called "Red the Rooster",
Wallace, James, or Howe, or King.
He was friendly, cheerful, handsome;
He could do most anything!

Didn't say just where he'd come from
With his clothes rolled in a tarp,
But he sang old songs and told good tales,
And danced as he played the mouth harp!

Joined us up west of Holbrook,
Had a grin that wouldn't quit.
Boss hired him on as rider
For that Aztec cow outfit

Which was often called the Hash Knife
For that controversial brand.
Tons of tough old Texas longhorns
And a million square of land.

The mercantile, A. and B. Schuster's,
Was robbed late one evening in May.
Ben fired at the redheaded robber;
Adolf saw the guy run away.

Whilst fixing breakfast, our cookie
Watched Red picking buckshot 'fore dawn,
By daybreak the kid was missing—
And four of our best horses gone.

He'd left a note for the brothers Schuster;
"I'm still carrying your lead:
But if you would kill this rooster,
You got to shoot him in the head!"

We learned he was wanted in Phoenix
For "borrowing" somebody's horse;
And that he'd broke jail down at Florence,
So he'z wanted there too, of course.

Turned up in New Mexico shortly;
At the French Ranch he stopped for awhile.
Will French thought him just a chuck liner,
But he liked the young cowpuncher's style

For he sang, and he danced for the waddies;
He stayed there well over a week.
Then Will found his Thoroughbred missing:
The stallion he'd named *Pow-a-Sheik.*

They trailed the daring young outlaw.
WANTED posters French posted about
New Mexico and Arizona—
And Old Mexico too, I've no doubt.

Then an envelope postmarked *Clifton*
Brought an altered poster which read
That "Due to a horse theft near Alma,"
Will French was now wanted by Red!

Old French was plumb flabbergasted;
Yet, he had to smile at the cheek
Of the rascally redheaded robber
Who'd stolen his fabulous Sheik.

The *Herald* over at St. Johns
Printed a verse that it had received;
To all of Red's earlier victims
Plus a sheriff he'd just deceived:

"I am the prince of the Aztec!
I'm perfection at robbing a store.
I've a stake left me by Wells Fargo;
Before long I'll have even more!

"The sheriff is wanting to kill me.
That sounds like a whole lot of fun!
'Tis strange that he hankers to drill me,
This red-headed sun of a gun.

"He handles a six-shooter neatly;
Gets a rabbit at nigh every pop.
Should the sheriff and I chance to meet up,
We'll have us an Arkansas hop!"

Red was seen once more in Holbrook,
Stole a horse and wrote to the press.
Rode north cross the reservation;
And the Holbrook paper professed:

"There's something to be admired in
Such dare-devil recklessness.
He's never shed another's blood
And his humor can't be suppressed."

Robbed a train in Colorado—
Called Fisher or Dayton by then.
But he, for a heist pulled at Ogden,
Wound up in the Utah State Pen.

Will French lost track of the outlaw,
But 'twas said that quite often he'd speak
Of the charming disarming young bandit
Who stole his Arabian Sheik:

French said, "Don't know where he is now,
But I'm sure if he served out his time,
He came out a-blowin, that mouth harp
Or spoutin, some dang silly rhyme

And dancin, a double shuffle
On the pavement, that cockatiel!
That rascally redheaded rooster,
That rhyming rogue, Red McNeil!

Swap Me A Biscuit (Performance Cut)

For historical notes on this poem, see uncut version in section IV.

I used to do some guidin'
Down on the lower Blue,
And Fred Martin was the finest cook
I think I ever knew.

His frijoles and his hash were great!
His dried apple pies, real fine!
(Claimed he crimped 'em with his old false teeth
'Cause that made the best design).

So when huntin' parties started out,
It was Fred we'd want for chuck,
And when we found that we would get him,
Well, we figgered, "We're in luck!"

'Cause what he made the very best—
Either wood stove or Dutch oven—
Was biscuits! Watch that crew come up
Just a-pushin' and a-shovin'

To get to ol' Fred's biscuits,
Of which we could eat right smart!
We'd rustle up some kindlin' wood
To give Fred a good head start.

One time we's camped at HU-Bar;
We'd packed in seven miles
To that little old log cabin.
Fred had done swept out the piles

Of trash and stuff the rats had left.
The place was smellin' great.
They's big thick steaks and chili beans
Boy, we could hardly wait!

But Fred, he said we'd have to stall
For just a few more minutes
"This oven just ain't heatin' right!"
And he keep peepin' in it.

"These biscuits, they ain't hardly browned!"
We kept hearin' that about 'em,
But we was starved and 'llowed as how
We'd have to eat without 'em.

And when at last he put 'em on
That rough old wood plank table,
He thought we'd woof 'em down real fast—
But none of us was able!

Them things was hard as dornicks!
We laughed and Chuck sez, "Shucks!
We could put 'em in our sling shots
And kill ourselves some bucks!"

Well, Fred, he was embarrassed,
Set the pan down on the floor,
And Slim took down that fiddle
That'd he'd hung up by the door.

Someone had brought "Jack Daniels";
We was drinkin' and a-smokin'
A-listenin' to the music,
Just a-visitin' and jokin',

When Tuffy put his finger up
And motioned us for quiet,
He pointed us to look that way,
Oh, brother, what a riot!

There was utter total silence;
Nobody said a word,
For there was a great big *pack rat*
A-totin' a dried horse turd!

He didn't seem to see us,
All he was lookin' at
Was that pan of Fred's cold biscuits,
What a feast for one pack rat!

Then we busted right out laughin',
And I reckon that rat heard,
'Cause he up and grabbed a biscuit
And he left his dried horse turd!

Poor Fred. He really got it!
We could not contain our mirth.
Red said, "Fred, there goes one biscuit—
You can see what it was worth!"

But I tell you, that warn't nothin'!
Back that rat come to the shack;
Quick, he up and grabbed his horse turd,
And he put Fred's biscuit back!

Vigilante Coming! (Performance Cut)

The performer must introduce the poem with notes from the uncut version in Section II.

The County Attorney refused to assist
In Rice's absurd little plan.
So hurrying down to the sheriff's house,
And lacking another good man,
Rice wakened the sheriff's beautiful wife,
Pauline Cushman, of Late-Great War fame,
Who was as well known for marksmanship
As her acting and spying could claim.

She hurriedly dressed and armed herself
With a Winchester rifle, and she,
When seated alone at the sheriff's desk,
Appeared just as calm as could be.
Rice went to the cells of his prisoners
And explaining the plan he'd devised,
He charged each man on his honor to stand,
And help him to save their own lives.

He would give all four of them rifles
Which would help fortify the small jail.
It would appear as if they were deputies
And if his shrewd plan didn't fail,
They would fool the wild vigilantes,
But when the fierce mob was quelled,
They must agree to give up the weapons
And return once more to their cells.

All agreed, and he took them upstairs—
Brash, Emerson, Dozier, and Dunn—
To the court room on the floor above;
There they waited until they'd begun
To hear the sound of loudly tramping feet
As the mob approached for assault.
Then Rice stuck his head out the window
And ordered the marchers to halt.

"I've got four well-armed deputies with me—
One more in the office below!"
Barrels of Winchester rifles appeared;
The advancing vanguard was slowed.
"You come at your peril, you blood-thirsty skunks!
And some of you soon will be dead
If you take just one more step forward," he yelled,
"We'll fill you all plumb full of lead!"

The effect was shock! That resolute flock
Scattered just like a covey of quail.
Rice, turning anew to his own motley crew,
Hoped the rest of his scheme wouldn't fail!
For there he sat till the August dawn
In that courtroom with four well armed men—
His erstwhile "prisoners"—and wondered, did he,
Just which idea would win:

The temptation to gain their *freedom*
Or their forsworn *honor* and *word.*
The one he feared most was Emerson,
Rough drifter, tough, hard-bitten bird.
Dozier and Dunn were neighborhood boys,
Young; had no offenses before,
They'd been hired by Brash to kill Joe White
In some local water rights war.

Rice told them all to give up their guns
And go peaceably back to their cells.
The two younger boys did just as he said,
But Brash didn't settle so well.
Then Emerson, placing his rifle
To the side of Brash's big head,
Just herded him back to the cell block,
Locked him in, and quietly, said,

"Come on, Mike, and get these two rifles,
I'm layin' 'em here on the floor.
You've treated us fair and I'm true to my word!"
And he closed and locked his cell door.
And what happened when the sheriff returned?
Some folks thought that Mike Rice should be fired.
He said, "The prisoners are safe in their cells.
That's the purpose for which I was hired!"

Bibliography

Adams, Ramon F. *Western Words*. Norman, OK, 1944.

Aguirre, Yjinio F. "The Last Days of the Dons," The Journal of Arizona History, 10:4 (Winter 1969), 239-255.

Anderson, Dorothy Daniels. *Arizona Legends and Lore: Tales of Southwestern Pioneers*. Phoenix, 1995.

"Anza Damns the Mission: A Spanish Soldier's Criticism of Indian Policy, 1772," ed. John L. Kessell. The Journal of Arizona History, XIII:1, (Spring 1972), 59.

Banks, Leo W. *"Big Nose Kate," Tombstone Chronicles: Tough Folks, Wild Times.* Phoenix, 1998.

Banks, Leo W. *"Bill Smith," Days of Destiny*, ed. Bob Albano. Phoenix, 1996, pp. 117-122.

Banks, Leo W. *"Johnny Behind the Deuce," Days of Destiny*, ed. Bob Albano. Phoenix, 1996, 17-22.

Banks, Leo W. *"The Lady in Blue," Arizona Highways*, (January 2001), 32-35.

Banks, Leo W. *Rattlesnake Blues: Dispatches From A Snakebit Territory*. Phoenix, 2000.

Barnes, Will C. *Apaches and Longhorns: The Reminiscences of Will C. Barnes.* Los Angeles, 1941.

Barnes, Will C. *Arizona Place Names*. Revised by Byrd H. Granger. Tucson, 1960.

Bell, Bob Boze. *"The Brothers Earp," Tombstone Chronicles: Tough Folks, Wild Times.* Phoenix, Arizona, 1998, 43-52.

Bell, Bob Boze. *The Illustrated Life & Times Of Wyatt Earp.* Cave Creek, Arizona, 1993, 34-36.

Bolton, Herbert Eugene. *The Padre on Horseback*, ed. John Francis Bannon, S.J. Chicago, 1963.

Bourke, John G. *"General Crook Visits the Supais, As Reported by John G. Bourke,"* ed. Frank E. Casanova, *Arizona and the West, A Quarterly Journal of History*, X:3 (Autumn 1968), 253-276.

Brophy, A. Blake. *"Fort Fillmore, N.M., 1861: Public Disgrace and Private Disaster," The Journal of Arizona History*, IX:4, (Winter 1968), 195-218.

Brown, Stan. "*Hashknife-Pony Express Ride as One,*" *Rim Country Echoes*, X:1 (January/February 1999), 2-3.

Brown, Stan. "*The History of The World's Oldest Continuous Rodeo.*" *Rim Review Rodeo Edition* (Payson, August 2000), 3.

Carlson, Lorri. Assistant Archivist, Sharlot Hall Museum, Prescott. Letter to the author, July 1997.

Cofer, Irene Cornwall. *The Lunch Tree*. Kingman, 1969.

"Commodore Perry Owens Tames the Wild, Wild West." *White Mountain Chronicles: A Historical Look at the White Mountains of Arizona*. Anonymous. Undated.

Conner, Ruth. "*Charlie Sam and the Sojourners,*" *The Journal of Arizona History,* XIV: 4 (Winter 1973), 303-315.

Conrad, David E., "*The Whipple Expedition in Arizona, 1853-1854,*" *Arizona and the West* II:2, 147-178.

Cook, Dean. "*Feather Duster Cowboy,*" *Arizona Born: Miscellaneous Minstrelsy*. Glendale, Arizona, 1998.

Cook, James E. *Arizona Republic* (May 22,1992), Phoenix, 1992.

Cookridge, E.H. *The Baron of Arizona*. New York, 1967.

Cowboy Reader, The. Eds. Lon Tinkle and Allen Maxweerll. New York, 1959.

Crutchfield, James A. *It Happened in Arizona*. Helena, MT, 1938.

Dary, David. *Cowboy Culture*. New York,1981.

Dedera, Don. "*Rev. Endicott Peabody,*" *Tombstone Chronicles*. Phoenix, 1998, 104-110.

DeWald, Louise. *Arizona Highways Heritage Cook Book*. Phoenix, 1994, 22.

Dillard, Gary. *Cochise County History Magazine*, I:1. (May 1997), 10-13.

Durham, Clarence W. *That Hashknife Kid*. City not stated, 1992.

Erbsen, Wayne. *Outlaw Ballads, Legends and Lore*. Asheville, NC, 1996.

Finch,Boyd. "*Sherod Hunter and the Confederates in Arizona,*" *The Journal of Arizona History*, X: 3 (Autumn 1969), 137-206.

Garate, Donald T. "*Who Named Arizona? The Basque Connection,*" *The Journal of Arizona History*, XXXX:1 (Spring 1999), 53-82.

"General Crook Visits the Supais, As Reported by John G. Bourke," ed. Frank E. Casanova, *Arizona and the West,* A Quarterly Journal of History, X:3 (Autumn, 1968), 253-276.

Glover, T.E. *The Lost Dutchman Mine of Jacob Waltz.* Phoenix,1998.

Goff, John S. *Arizona: An Illustrated History of the Grand Canyon State.* Northridge, CA, 1988.

Goff, John S. *Arizona Biographical Dictionary*, Cave Creek, Arizona, 1983, 91.

Grammer, Betty Chambliss. *"Jes Burke," Down on the Blue: Blue River, 1878-1986.* ed. Cleo Cosper Coor, Goodyear, 1992, 24.

Gray, Robert S. Phd., Professor of geology, Santa Barbara City College. Letter to the author, April 16, 2002.

Hall, Sharlot. *Cactus and Pine*. Prescott, 1989.

Hanchett, Leland J., Jr. *Arizona's Graham Tewksbury Feud,* Phoenix, 1994.

Hanchett, Leland J., Jr. *Black Mesa*. Phoenix, 1996.

Hanchett, Leland J., Jr. *Crooked Trail to Holbrook*. Phoenix, 1993.

Hausman, Gerald. *Meditation With the Navajo*. Santa Fe, 1987.

Horan, James D. and Paul Sann. *Pictorial History of the Wild West*. New York, 1954, 103-115, 131.

Ives, Ronald L. *"Kino's Exploration of the Pinacate Region," Journal of Arizona History*, 7:2 (Summer 1966), 59-75.

Jackson, Susan, Executive Director, Prescott Fine Arts Association, Prescott, Arizona. Letter to the author, July 1997.

Jett, William Bladen. *"The Reluctant Corporal," The Autobiography of William Bladen Jett*, pt.2, ed. Henry P. Walker, *The Journal of Arizona History*, XII (Summer 1971), 112-144.

Kammer, Jerry. *"Visitors Find Magic in Land of Havasupai," The Arizona Republic* (May 17, 1998), T-1.

Kessell, John L. *"Anza, Indian Fighter: The Spring Campaign of 1766," The Journal of Arizona History*, IX (Autumn 1968), 55-163.

Langley, Dana. "The Indestructibles," *Arizona Highways*, August 1968, 8-13, 29-35.

Lambert, Elizabeth Wood. *Arizona Hoof Trails*. Portland, 1956.

Lauer, Charles D. *Old West: Adventures in Arizona*. Phoenix, 1989, 102-103.

Lauer, Charles D. *Tales of Arizona Territory*. Phoenix, 1995.

Looney, Ralph and Bruce Dale. "*Indians of North America: The Navajo.*" *National Geographic*, 142:6 (December 1972), 741.

McCarty, Lea F. *The Gunfighters*. Berkeley, 1959.

McDermott, Edwin J., S.J. "*The Saga of Father Kino,*" *Arizona Highways* (March 1961), 6-29.

Martin, John F. *The Havasupai*. Flagstaff, 1990.

Martin, Judy. *Arizona Walls*. Phoenix, 1997.

Mason, Robert. *The Burning,* Phoenix, 2000.

Mason, Robert. Letter to the author, March 2001.

Mason, Robert. *Verde Valley Lore.* Rio Verde, Arizona, 1997.

Metz, Leon C. "*Gunslingers and the Art of Gunfighting,*" *Wild West*, (April 1998), 28-34.

Miller, Warren, Curator of Education, Sharlott Hall Museum, Prescott, Arizona. Letter to the author, March 1997.

Moore, Dan. *Shoot Me a Biscuit*. Tucson, 1974.

Moore, Dan. *Short Stories of the Southwest*. Casa Grande, 1980.

Moulton, Candy. *The Writers Guide to Everyday Life in the 1800s*. Cincinnati, 1993.

Moulton, Candy. *The Writer's Guide to Everyday Life in the Wild West.* Cincinnati, 1999.

Muehl, Chips. *Buckskins, Bedbugs & Bacon*. Phoenix, 2001.

Neal, Grace. *That Cowboy From Burro Creek*. Kingman, 1993.

Officer, James E. "*Kino and Agriculture in the Pimería Alta,*" *The Journal of Arizona History* 34:3 (Autumn 1993), 291-295.

O'Neal, Bill. *The Arizona Rangers*. Austin, TX, 1987.

Polzer, Charles, S.J. *A Kino Guide: His Missions—His Monuments*. Tucson, 1968.

Powell, Donald M. "*The Baron of Arizona Self-Revealed: A Letter to his Lawyer in 1894.*" *Arizona and the West, A Quarterly Journal of History*, I:2, (Summer 1959), 161-173.

Powell, Donald M. *The Peralta Grant: James Addison Reavis and the Barony of Arizona.* (Norman, OK, 1960).

Redondo, Margaret Proctor. "*Valley of Iron*," *The Journal of Arizona History*, XXXIV: 3 (Autumn 1993), 233-274.

Roberts, Paul H. *Them Were the Days*. San Antonio, 1965.

Ronstadt, Federico Jose Maria. *Borderman: Memoirs of Federico Jose Maria Ronstadt*, ed. Edward F. Ronstadt. Albuquerque, 1993.

Ruffner, Lester Ward "Budge," *Shot in the Ass With Pesos*. Tucson, 1979.

Smalley, George H. "*Climax Jim, My Favorite Outlaw*," *Arizona Highways* (April 1949), 36-39.

Starkey, Larry. "*Buckskin Frank Leslie*," *Days of Destiny*. Phoenix, 1996, 6-16.

Steber, Rick. *Gunfighters*. Prineville, OR, 1998.

Stocker, Joseph. "*Arizona's Fabulous Baron*," *Arizona Highways* (August 1960), 32-39.

Stocker, Joseph. "*City of Lost Hope*," *Arizona Highways*, (May 1961), 36-39.

Swearengin, John A. *Good Men, Bad Men, Law Men*. Florence, 1991.

Tinsley, Jim Bob. *Hash Knife Brand*. Gainesville, FL, 1993.

Tinsley, Jim Bob. *He Was Singin' This Song*. Orlando, 1981, 186-188.

Traywick, Ben T. "*Tombstone's Bird Cage*," *Wild West*, October 1994, 58-64, 96-97.

Trimble, Marshall. *Arizona, A Cavalcade of History*. Tucson, 2000.

Trimble, Marshall. *Arizona Adventure!* Phoenix, 1996.

Trimble, Marshall. *Arizoniana: Stories From Old Arizona*. Scottsdale, 1988.

Trimble, Marshall. *In Old Arizona*. Phoenix, 1993.

Trimble, Marshall. *The Law of the Gun*. Phoenix, 1999.

Trimble, Marshall. "*The Legend of the Bill Smith Gang*," *The Arizona Republic*, June 30, 1985, Arizona Section, 22.

Turner, D.L. "*Shepherded by Sinners and Saints Alike: A Tale of Mormons, Outlaws, and Sheepman in Northern Arizona*," *The Journal of Arizona History*, XXXIX:3 (Autumn 1998), 225-234.

Walker, Henry P. and Don Bufkin. *Historical Atlas of Arizona*, second edition, (Norman, OK 1986), 45.

Walker, Henry Pickering. "*Preacher in Helldorado,*" *The Journal of Arizona History*, XV:(Autumn 1974), 223-238.

Wallace, Jerry. "*How the Episcopal Church Came to Arizona,*" *The Journal of Arizona History*, VI: 3, 101-115.

Watts, Peter. *A Dictionary of the Old West*. NY, 1987.

Wolk, Allen and W.Nyack. *Gunfighters of the West.* New York, 1994.

Woods, Dan. *Short Stories of the Southwest.* Casa Grande, 1980.

Wright, Barton. Director Emeritus, Museum of Northern Arizona, Letter to the author, March 2001.

Zachariae, Barbara. "*Pleasant Valley Days: A History of the People of Pleasant Valley.*" Young, Arizona, 1991.

Index

Order Form

☐ Yes! Please send me the following title.

Name ____
Address ____
City_______________State _______________Zip _______________
Phone________________________Fax __________________________

Title	Qty.	Each	Total
Arizona Herstory. Tales From Her Storied Past. By Dee Strickland Johnson. Foreword by Marshall Trimble.	_____	$19.95	_____
	Subtotal		_____
Please add $4.50 for the first item, plus $1.00 for each additional item for shipping and handling.	S&H		_____
Foreign orders must be accompanied by a postal money order in U.S. funds.	**TOTAL**		_____

Send check or money order to:
Dee Strickland Johnson
HC 3 Box 593-F
Payson, AZ 85541

To order by phone call (928) 474-8305. Contact us about discounts.